DANIELLE BEAN

You Are Enough

What Women of the Bible Teach You About Your Mission and Worth

ASCENSION

West Chester, Pennsylvania

Nihil obstat: Rev. Robert A. Pesarchick, STD
                   Censor librorum
                   February 15, 2019

Imprimatur: +Most Rev. Charles J. Chaput, O.F.M. Cap.
                   Archbishop of Philadelphia
                   February 21, 2019

Ascension
Post Office Box 1990
West Chester, PA 19380
1-800-376-0520
ascensionpress.com

Cover design: Rosemary Strohm

Printed in the United States of America
   22 23 24 25 9 8 7 6

ISBN 978-1-945179-48-8

CONTENTS

INTRODUCTION

I'll just come out and say it: The Old Testament is pretty weird.

For me anyway, reading the New Testament, the stories of Jesus' life, the places he went, and the words he spoke, is a much more accessible source of inspiration. When I wrote my last book, *You're Worth It,* which focused on Jesus' real-life interactions with real women in the New Testament, I found many ancient women I could readily relate to. Their stories of struggle, hard work, and faith in the face of great difficulty are moving, relatable, and encouraging. Thinking of these women, standing in the physical presence of Jesus, God made man, our loving Teacher and all-giving Savior, was a deeply moving exercise.

But women of the Old Testament? Women who lived long before Jesus, in times and places where things like polygamy and incest were common? Where people cut off each other's heads and worshiped golden calves and slew giants and sold siblings into slavery? Who exactly were these women and what relevance could their stories possibly have for us today?

Lots.

As a cradle Catholic, I have read and heard others read aloud, many stories from the Old Testament hundreds of times over the course of my life. As I did research for this book, however, I read many of these familiar stories with fresh perspective. And I was surprised.

There, in the sometimes odd, sometimes colorful stories of our age-old sisters in the Old Testament, there in those ancient words, I found an eternal and tangible truth: Our God is a good God and a patient God, and he has an abundance of love for his people. *God loves us.*

God has a unique love and a unique plan, not only for all women, but for every woman in particular. That means you. That means me. He calls each of us to play a particular role in this life, one that he equips us for and loves us through, steadfast and faithful, every step of the way. Only you can answer your calling.

Now you might think you already know this stuff. God loves us and calls us to holiness, *yeah I know, blah, blah, blah* ... but do you really know it? Do you let yourself really know it?

Can you take that simple phrase—*God loves me*—and let it travel from where you know it in your head, all the way down to your heart? Can you know and accept God's love—really know it—in your heart?

That's what this book is all about.

Some of the women we will meet in the pages ahead are very different from you and me. Some of their lives and circumstances might seem impossibly strange from our modern perspectives, but they are real. Their stories are real. Though some details might differ, the stories of their struggles to know God's love, to trust, to hear his call, and to find love, healing, hope, and acceptance are the same stories we live out today.

There is so much about our modern world and many of our personal circumstances that might leave us feeling alone, unloved, and powerless. I don't know the details of your struggles, but God does. I don't know the particular ways God is calling you to know him, love him, and find peace and lasting joy in this life and the next by answering your unique call to holiness. I do know he is calling you.

God is calling you to greatness. He made you for it.

He is calling you just as he called Rahab, Abigail, Bathsheba, Tamar, Judith, Delilah, Hannah, Sarah, Miriam, Ruth, Rachel, Leah, Naomi, and the dozens of other women we are going to meet in the pages ahead.

It is my hope and my prayer that you will join me in reading the stories of these women and begin to see and feel the eternal truth of God's love in a new way. In a way that will allow you to dig deep into these age-old stories of our sisters from long ago and begin to see a story of your own, a story of God's unique love for you and the unique calling he made you for.

You—with all your weaknesses and flaws—were made for this. You—in all of your struggles and pain—are enough.

Do you believe that? Most of us don't completely understand or accept that, but that's why we are here. That's why we are meeting here in these humble pages.

We are here to learn the truth of God's infinite love and then relearn it. We are here so we can know God's love and accept it in our hearts, and then when we forget it, we are here to remind each other. We are here to repeat and affirm the truth of God's love for each of us as individuals and for all women as a gift to humanity—as many times as we need to. We are here to do these things until the truth of God's love finally seeps through our thick skin and finds a home in our hearts and we keep it there.

Are you ready? There are some fascinating stories I want you to hear. There are some beautiful, strong, trustworthy, hardworking, faith-filled, and inspiring women I want you to meet. And there is an eternal truth of God's infinite love

I want you to find written inside these women's stories that matches an eternal truth written deep inside your own heart:

God loves you. God calls you. He made you for greatness, and you are enough.

Let's find out what that can mean as we explore our own unique experiences and our eternal stories, together.

Chapter One

GOD CALLS YOU IN

God Calls You ... Just as You Are

TRYING OUT AND FITTING IN

When I was in sixth grade, one of my best friends was a girl named Katie. Katie had all the things. Stylish clothes, shiny blonde hair, cute freckles, a "perfect" family of a mom, dad, and two older sisters, and a magnetic personality. Her father drove a sports car, and their family lived in a beautiful house on the end of a country road (with an in-ground pool in the backyard!).

Katie was fun to be around, and I was happy she considered me "cool" enough to be her friend. She invited me to sleepovers and pool parties, and I did my best to keep up with the other girls at these events. They were pretty girls. Popular girls. Confident girls.

They were cheerleaders.

I realized pretty quickly that I was the only one among them not practicing dance moves or flips and not talking about what happened at the last game (when that cute older football player had stopped to talk with Gerilyn, and how he had flirted with her, and how all the other girls just *could not believe it*).

I assessed my situation, my feeling of being on the "outside," despite what appeared to be my friend Katie's acceptance, and decided there was only one thing to do: I needed to become a cheerleader.

Tryouts took place over the course of several days in an old community building with a wooden dance floor. The cheerleading coaches were not moms; they were stunning young women who knew exactly how to wear makeup and tie their hair up in bouncy ponytails. Wannabe cheerleaders were given numbers to pin on our shirts. We broke up into smaller groups, each with a leader who taught us a dance routine.

I was not much of a dancer, but I was focused. I concentrated on the way the leader moved, the way her arms floated gracefully through the air, and the way her feet sashayed her body effortlessly across the room, seemingly without ever touching the floor.

I attempted to recreate the routine. The only problem was that I had to use my own body to do it—my arms that seemed to flail more than float and my feet that hit the wooden floor with a gratuitous amount of noise and commotion.

Thank goodness for the gymnastics. Thanks to countless hours spent flipping around my backyard at home with the neighborhood kids, I could do a cartwheel, a handstand, a backbend, and even a reasonably decent-looking back handspring.

Over several days of tryouts, I struggled through the dance routines and did my best to shine through the gymnastics. I also paid careful attention to my clothing choices and hairstyle. I noticed that the older girls did not wear sweatpants, as I had to our first day of tryouts. They wore athletic shorts and slouchy sweatshirts over fitted tank tops. Their wide-necked sweatshirts would sometimes hang off one shoulder, creating a look of "casual cool." I did my best to adapt my own wardrobe to these standards, and I pinned my hair up with ribbons and barrettes I borrowed from my older sister.

And my efforts paid off. I made the first cut. Only half the girls were invited to the final day of tryouts, and I was one of them. I was elated! I dreamed of a crimson red cheerleader jacket with my name embroidered on it.

FACING THE TRUTH

I was trying so hard to fit in, and my ultimate goal of becoming a cheerleader seemed so obviously important to me, that I was surprised by something my mother asked as she drove me to the final day of tryouts.

"Why do you want to do this?" she asked. "These girls are different from Stacie."

She was right. My very best friend, at least before I became friends with Katie, was a quiet, more studious type like me. Stacie did not wear bouncy ponytails or slouchy sweatshirts. She and I loved to read and talk about our favorite books. We spent hours lying on the floor in her bedroom, side by side, drawing fantastic scenes with colored pencils. I had been so busy with tryouts, though, that I hadn't talked to Stacie much lately.

I don't remember how I answered my mother that day, but something in her questioning made me pause. It made me think about who I really was and the different person I was trying to be. But I stopped short of admitting the full truth to myself: *I am not a cheerleader.*

At the end of tryouts that day, my name was not on the list of girls who had made the final cut. That list of new cheerleaders, pinned on the wall outside the building, spoke a truth to me that my mother had only hinted at, and that I had not wanted to admit to myself: *You are not a cheerleader.*

Those words stung. Not because I enjoyed awkwardly attempting to keep up in group dance routines, but because they excluded me. I felt alone in my gangly body and not-quite-slouchy-enough sweatshirt. Here, in this place, I did not fit in. I did not belong.

You may never have wanted to be a cheerleader, but you probably have a memory of a time when you felt a similar way. I'm sure we would all like to dismiss stories like these as merely the trials of adolescence, but the truth is that the feeling of not fitting in comes back to sting us on a regular basis, even long after high school graduation.

I feel it when I am sitting alone on the bleachers at my son's baseball game and all the other moms appear to be lifelong friends, laughing and chatting loudly about people and places I don't know. I feel it when I bump into a friend at the gas station who is wearing a stylish new jacket, and I suddenly notice my own coat is dingy and covered with dog hair. I feel it when I browse Facebook and see photos of a group of people I know, smiling and clinking glasses at a social event I didn't know about—because I wasn't invited.

BELONGING MATTERS

It might be tempting to think that these are trivial, petty problems, and that we need to just grow up and get over them, but they are more than that.

Human beings are social creatures. Belonging is important. Having a sense of who we are, feeling truly free to be who we are, and finding acceptance are instinctual drives. It hurts us, at the very core of our being, in ways many of us are afraid to closely examine, to feel like we don't fit in.

Do you ever feel like you don't fit in? Maybe your marriage is failing, and you feel like you are the only one struggling. Maybe you didn't get the job you wanted, or were afraid to even apply for it, for fear of not being "enough." Maybe you feel abandoned and rejected by your grown children. Maybe you weren't invited to be a part of your close friend's wedding and cannot understand why. Maybe your own sister never seems to have time to spend with you, despite the fact that you text her daily.

Maybe you feel awkward in your body. Maybe you wonder how other women know how to shop for the right clothes and seem to be so sure of themselves. Maybe you feel like everyone else is in on a secret they are not sharing with you. A secret about how to have fun, how to fit in, and how to be accepted. Maybe you think you are the only one left on the outside, wondering why you are different, and why you can't seem to figure out how to be truly happy in life.

Many of us feel this way. In fact, if you do not ever feel like an outsider, go ahead and close this book right now and put it in the nearest trash can.

OK, is it just us now? The outsiders? An ironic name for our group, because there are a lot of us here in it. Everyone, if they are truthful, will admit that they suffer from feeling alone and rejected sometimes. Everyone feels awkward and like they don't fit in sometimes.

The good news is that this very human condition so many of us suffer from is not the end of the story. We don't have to stay here. The good news for those of us who ever feel too old, too young, too fat, too thin, too smart, too dumb, too silly, too serious, too focused, too distracted, too rich, or too poor to truly fit in is that we don't need to change who we are to belong.

You don't need to be anyone other than your authentic self to be enough.

God, our Father in heaven, sees you just as you are and calls you to great things. He knows your flaws, your weaknesses, your quirks, your worries, your struggles, your anxieties, and all those things you try to hide about yourself because they make you "different," and still he calls you. He sees all the messed up and broken things about you that sometimes lead you to discouragement and despair, and yet he is not discouraged.

He who made you calls you to great things.

It's OK if you don't see that yet. It can be hard to see God's plan and the truth of God's love in your own story. Let's start instead by looking at some other women's stories. Let's find out how God has called women who were "outsiders" to great things throughout all of history. Some of the most compelling of these stories star our ancient "sisters" and "girlfriends" from the Old Testament of the Bible who were women who did not fit in. They did not seem to "belong." Yet God saw them, God knew them, and he called them his.

RAHAB, THE OUTSIDER

Let's begin with Rahab. You won't find a more obvious outsider than a sneaky prostitute, after all. That's right. Rahab was a prostitute, but God knew she was capable of great things, and he called her to play an important, honored role in the history of our salvation.

We meet Rahab in the book of Joshua, where she is described as a "harlot" who lives in Jericho. Rahab was a businesswoman who ran an inn where travelers would stop for food and overnight accommodations. The word "harlot," of course, means that she offered sexual services as well.

In any culture, women who sell themselves for sex are considered part of a dishonorable, lower class, and indeed, the Ten Commandments affirm the seriousness of sexual sin.

What the Bible does not tell us, though, are the extenuating circumstances under which someone like Rahab might have chosen this way of life. She might have been born into poverty. She might have been abused and abandoned by a bad husband. She might have lost her parents at a young age and had no means of providing for herself. Women don't choose the degradation of prostitution, and inevitable social rejection, when there are other, more attractive options available.

In addition to social rejection, it would be reasonable to consider that Rahab likely suffered from a lack of self-esteem as well. We women, whether we recognize sexual sin for the evil that it is or not, suffer psychological wounds when we misuse our bodies and allow others to misuse them for sex. More so for women than for men, sex is undeniably attached to love, commitment, and relationship. When we use something as intimate and powerful as sex outside of that context, we hurt ourselves. Whether she knew it or not, Rahab was hurting herself.

RAHAB STEPS OUT IN FAITH

So when the Bible tells us that Rahab was a "harlot," we can deduce that she would have been a wounded and unhappy woman, a second-class citizen and an outsider, even among her own people. In other words, Rahab did not fit in; in her own way, she was not a cheerleader.

As such, Rahab was not exactly the kind of person most of us would expect to play a significant role in salvation history—or someone we would expect to have the honor of being named in the genealogy of Jesus. But these things happened. God sees beyond our human limitations and has plans that we do not understand.

Let's see what happened.

In the book of Joshua, we read that Joshua, the leader of the Israelites, has sent two men as spies into the land of Jericho to scope it out and make plans for an attack. These two men stay with Rahab. The king of Jericho receives word of these spies and their whereabouts, and he calls on Rahab to turn the men in.

Rahab, like many of her people, knows the story of the parting of the Red Sea. But unlike many of her people, Rahab has faith in the one true God, whom she recognizes as the God of the Israelites. As such, she does not turn in the spies but chooses to help them instead. She hides the men under the flax on her roof and tells her king:

> True, men came to me, but I did not know where they came from; and when the gate was to be closed, at dark, the men went out; where the men went I do not know; pursue them quickly, for you will overtake them (Joshua 2:4-5).

She lies! Rahab explains her actions to the spies she helps by giving testimony to her faith in the strength and goodness of God:

> [She] said to the men, "I know that the LORD has given you the land, and that the fear of you has fallen upon us, and that all the inhabitants of the land melt away before you. For we have heard how the LORD dried up the water of the Red Sea before you when you came out of Egypt, and what you did to the two kings of the Amorites that were beyond the Jordan, to Sihon and Og, whom you utterly destroyed. And as soon as we heard it, our hearts melted, and there was no courage left in any man, because of you; for the LORD your God is he who is God in heaven above and on earth beneath" (Joshua 2:9-11).

A GLIMPSE OF JESUS

In exchange for the favor of helping them, Rahab asks the spies to spare her and her family when the Israelites return to attack the city of Jericho. The men agree, and they give her a scarlet cord to hang outside her window. The cord is to serve as a sign to the attacking Israelites to spare Rahab and her family, who will be hiding inside.

This marking of a residence with the color red calls to mind the story of the Passover, when, in accordance with God's instructions, Moses commanded the Israelites to mark their homes with the blood of a sacrificial lamb or goat as a sign that the "angel of death" should pass over their residences when striking down the Egyptians, who held them as slaves.

In the story of the Passover and in the story of Rahab and the spies, the blood of the lamb and the scarlet cord are powerful symbols of something yet to come. That something is the blood of Jesus, the Lamb of God, the Savior who is yet to come to save all from death and sin.

In living out the small details of her own story, Rahab could not have known this, but she did know God, and she trusted in his goodness with simple faith. God saw that faith, and he rewarded it, not only by sparing her life but by giving her a role to play in foreshadowing the coming of the Savior. Her simple story of faith and redemption was significant enough to be detailed in the Bible for all future generations, including us, to read about.

WE ARE ALL CALLED

Why would God want us to read this story?

Well, do you ever feel unworthy of God's love because you are a sinner? Do you ever think that things you have done in the past, or maybe even some things that are part of your life right now, make you unfit to do great things for God?

I think we all feel that way sometimes. It's tempting to think that we are too messed up, too broken, or too weak to do God's work. Rahab's story is a reminder to us all that we do not have to be perfect for God to use us in significant ways. He sees you right now, exactly as you are, and calls you to draw closer to him. God the Father, who made you and knows you intimately, inside and out, calls you to do his will. No one is beyond redemption, and no one has gone too far astray to experience the saving power of God's love. None of us is perfect, yet each of us is called.

ABIGAIL, THE LOYAL WIFE

Sometimes it's not our own sin but the sins of others that make us feel like outsiders and that make us doubt our own goodness and worth. One notable example of this is the story of Abigail, whom we meet in the first book of Samuel. Abigail is a virtuous woman, described as beautiful and intelligent, the wife of a wealthy sheep rancher.

It might sound like Abigail has it pretty good, being one of the beautiful people, part of a wealthy class, but wait until you hear about her husband, Nabal. "Nabal" means "fool," and that is an apt description for the man Abigail has had the misfortune of marrying.

The entire dramatic story is wrapped up neatly in a single chapter of the Bible. We read that David, the future king, calls on Nabal to send food to his men in the field who are in need of supplies. This is not so much a request for a favor as for repayment of a debt. David's men had previously helped Nabal care for and protect his sheep, and now, when they are in need of supplies, it seems a convenient time to ask for payment in the form of food.

Nabal, however, who is described as harsh and bad-mannered, refuses to send food to David's men. Instead, he grows indignant at the request:

> And Nabal answered David's servants, "Who is David? Who is the son of Jesse? There are many servants nowadays who are breaking away from their masters. Shall I take my bread and my water and my meat that I have killed for my shearers, and give it to men who come from I do not know where?" So David's young men turned away, and came back and told him all this (1 Samuel 25:10-12).

As you can imagine, David does not appreciate this response. He himself grows indignant, and he prepares his men to attack the entire household of Nabal in an act of vengeance for this offense. Nabal's servants hear of this, and in fear for their lives, they run to Abigail to tell her what her husband has done.

STANDING UP FOR VIRTUE

Poor Abigail. As the wife of a harsh and bad-mannered man, she is probably used to cleaning up her husband's messes. It is probably embarrassing and even personally devastating at times. She herself is likely the victim of Nabal's bad temper and brash behavior. Yet Abigail remains loyal to her foolish husband and determines to do her best to make things right.

It is likely that Nabal's men go to Abigail in their fear because they know she is a strong woman of virtue, and that she alone has the power to smooth things over. Nabal is a stubborn fool, and David is a hot-headed, impulsive man. Abigail, intelligent and beautiful, is the only one who can bring about peace in this terrible circumstance.

Does Abigail feel afraid and alone when she finds herself stuck between two violent, angry men? Does she wonder at the injustice of her situation? Does being the only person who will stand up for peace and virtue in a world where few others are keeping their heads make her feel like an outsider?

She probably does not feel that way or let any of that slow her down.

Abigail orders her husband's men to prepare a large amount of food, and then, without telling her husband, she herself sets out to meet the powerful and angry David and his four hundred men, who are intent on destroying her household.

She greets David by falling on her knees at his feet. Then, in an impressively diplomatic and persuasive speech, Abigail begs David to lay all the guilt for her husband's misdeeds upon herself instead. She praises David for his virtue and calls on God to bless him. She reminds him of his own goodness and his own power to choose good over evil, and she ends by predicting that David will be a gracious and virtuous king when he returns to power:

> Please forgive the trespass of your handmaid; for the LORD will certainly make my lord a sure house, because my lord is fighting the battles of the LORD; and evil shall not be found in you so long as you live (1 Samuel 25:28).

Abigail does not accuse David of sinful pride or of seeking a disordered sense of revenge, though those would be accurate descriptions of his behavior. David has been wronged, after all, but his dispute is with Nabal, not the hundreds of innocent people who would be killed in a rampage against Nabal's household.

David is so impressed by Abigail's words and actions that not only does he call off his men, but when Nabal dies shortly afterward, he sends for Abigail and makes her one of his wives. Abigail, who stands up bravely in the face of violence and demonstrates humility, generosity, and virtue when no one else dares, finds herself married at last to a man who respects her. Her virtue brings her a happier life than the one she has previously known.

GOD SEES YOU WHERE YOU ARE

Do you ever feel alone under difficult circumstances you face? Do you ever feel that no one sees you and no one knows or understands the kinds of challenges you face? We all feel that way sometimes, and although the details of our circumstances might be different, Abigail's story gives hope to every one of us who ever suffers loneliness as a victim of others' bad behavior or as the lone voice in a battle against evil.

Abigail was married to a bad man, and she found herself in an unfair situation, but she did not let her circumstances determine her future. Like Rahab, she knew the truth, and she dared to speak the truth and do the right thing, even though it must have been a terrifying thing to do.

Both Rahab and Abigail took courageous, heroic action in a world where women were unlikely heroes. But God saw them. He saw them in their broken, mixed up lives, and he called upon them to do big things. The things they did were so big, they wound up being written about in the Bible, so that, thousands of years later, the names of Rahab and Abigail might be read and their stories might be remembered. These stories share a message that God has for us—and for you.

Perhaps you think you are an unlikely hero in your world today. Perhaps you feel too weak and sinful or too trapped and alone to do anything important. Well, Rahab and Abigail are here to tell you those things are no excuse.

God sees you where you are. He knows you exactly as you are, and he calls you to greatness anyway. What will your story be?

CLOSING PRAYER

Lord, grant that I may always allow myself to be guided by you, always follow your plans, and perfectly accomplish your holy will. Grant that in all things, great and small, today and all the days of my life, I may do whatever you require of me. Help me respond to the slightest prompting of your grace, so that I may be your trustworthy instrument for your honor. May your Will be done in time and in eternity—by me, in me, and through me. Amen.

– St. Teresa of Avila

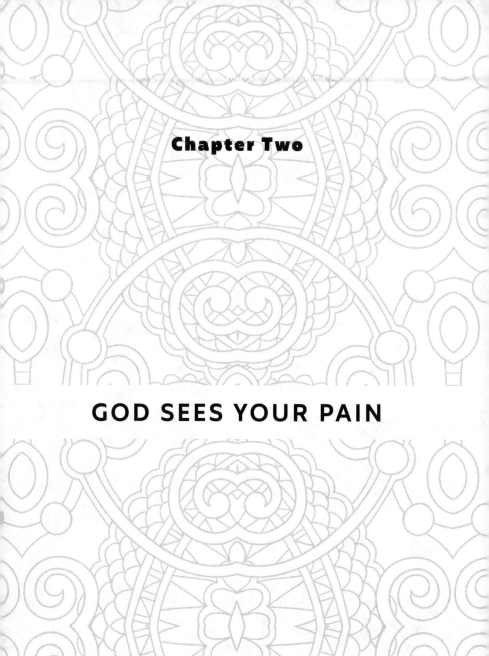

Chapter Two

GOD SEES YOUR PAIN

God Acknowledges Your Suffering and Lifts You Up

BONDING IN BATHROOMS

She was huddled in the corner near the hand dryers when I first saw her. Smudges of mascara stained her eyes and cheeks. Her hair hung in strands over her face, falling loose from a messy bun. She was wearing a black dress and clutching a pair of heels in her hands. Her arms were crossed over her knees as she hugged them to her chest.

I was attending a concert in a large stadium and had just waited in a long line to use the ladies' restroom. I was washing my hands when I saw her there. Paper towels littered the tiles around her as she sat, all alone, in a crowd.

She stared at the wall until I came close enough for her to notice me. I bent down beside her, and she turned to me with swollen eyes.

"Are you OK?" I asked, "Do you need some help?"

She sniffed and shook her head. "I'm fine," she said. "Just not going back out there."

"Out where?"

"Out where *he* is." She nodded toward the exit door.

"Boyfriend?" I asked.

She nodded and covered her face with her hands.

I stayed and asked more questions. She told me that there had been a disagreement and it had turned ugly. It always seemed to turn ugly when he was drinking, she sobbed, and she didn't know how to make it stop. They lived together, and he kept saying they would get married, but it never seemed to happen. She wanted to have a family but wasn't sure what kind of father he would make, and so she was thinking about leaving but was too scared to make such a difficult, life-changing decision.

It's amazing what you can hear in a ladies' room, if you take the time to listen.

I helped her call her sister and arrange for a ride home. I know I only heard one side of the story, but I also know I met a wounded woman that night. Whatever the details of her relationship with her boyfriend, she was hurt by him and found herself in a place no one wants to be: sitting on a dirty bathroom floor, telling her sad story and crying her eyes out to a stranger.

These are the kinds of things that happen in ladies' rooms. Especially at places like bars and concerts, especially where people are drinking, wounded women often connect with one another in the ladies' room. We share tissues and sob stories. We give advice and ask for opinions.

Some friends and I once counseled a young woman we did not know, as we brushed our hair and freshened our lip gloss, that if a guy was unwilling to bring her around his friends and only called her for "dates" late at night when he was bored and lonely, he probably was not a keeper. She seemed genuinely grateful for our mothering that night.

I once ran into an entire bridal party in a ladies' room. Upon learning that I was married more than twenty years, they kept me there, grilling me with questions about love, sex, communication, and personal relationships. We took a photo together before returning to the restaurant. I still wonder if I wound up in someone's scrapbook that night.

A friend once told me she wondered if one day in heaven she would meet up again with all the random women she had bonded with in bathrooms over the years. I laughed at the idea, but it made me realize that this is something we women do.

Like the woman at the concert who fought with her boyfriend, when things get rough, we escape to the ladies' room. We look for safety and understanding among our sisters. We share stories and sympathy because even though we are all different, many of our experiences are the same. Human beings are flawed creatures. So many women are hurt in their relationships with men.

"ME TOO"

Sometimes, in ladies' room conversations, or even among close friends, we wait for others to open up before allowing ourselves to be vulnerable, too. Once someone dares to let her guard down and share her struggles or show that she is hurting, she is often met with a chorus of, "Me too."

"Me too" is the stuff that bonding is made of.

This is why the "Me Too" movement in our culture, a campaign encouraging women to share their experiences and speak out against sexual harassment and assault, resonates with women from all walks of life. Of course, not all men are abusers and not all women have suffered sexual harassment or violence. Yet we as a culture must face the fact that an alarming number of women hear stories of manipulative, abusive, powerful men taking advantage of others and respond with, "Me too."

BEING HEARD

There is a lot of healing to be found in sharing our stories and listening to one another. Sometimes the most painful part of what a woman experiences as a victim of a bad relationship or sexual harassment or assault is feeling all alone in it, thinking that no one sees her pain, no one sees her suffering, and no one hears her story. Some women who speak out even run the risk of not being believed or of being blamed for their abuse.

I haven't met up with you in the ladies' room yet, so I don't know your story. But every woman has a story to share.

You might be in a relationship with a bad man who doesn't treat you well. You might be in a relationship with a good man who is nevertheless imperfect, and so he sometimes hurts you anyway. You might carry the burden of a wounded sexual past that leaves you feeling broken and mistrustful of men. Whatever the details, all of us sometimes find ourselves like the woman I met at the concert, sitting alone, feeling used up, rejected, and unseen. All of us can hear another woman's story of suffering and, on some level, respond with a heartbroken, "Me too."

No matter what you may have suffered in your life or are currently suffering, big things or small things, important things or trivial things, you can know this: God the Father, who sees all things and knows all things, sees you in your suffering. He sees your story, he knows your story, and he values your voice. You are his precious daughter, and he affirms your dignity and worth. Your story is important, and God wants to give it the hearing it deserves.

You might wonder how we can know God sees us in our pain. How can we know he cares? Well, we can start by listening to the stories of women who went before us, some of our sisters in the Old Testament who lived thousands of years ago. Let's take a look at how some of these women suffered at the hands of men and how God saw them, heard them, and allowed their stories to be told, long before "me too" was even a thing.

BATHSHEBA, USED BY A KING

We find Bathsheba's story in the second book of Samuel. It's a familiar one to many as its salacious details make it quite memorable.

King David, we are told, is walking on the roof of his house one afternoon, when he sees a beautiful woman bathing below. It is Bathsheba. He lusts after her, and without knowing anything else about her, he decides he must have her. He finds out who she is, sends for her, and has sex with her. Then he is done with her. Just like that.

"So David sent messengers, and took her; and she came to him, and he lay with her ... Then she returned to her house" (2 Samuel 11:4).

Some romance, right? The fact that the passage does not tell us whether Bathsheba, who is married to another man, consents to sex with David, is telling in itself. It is not mentioned because it does not appear to matter. David is the actor in every line in the telling of this story. He lusts after her, he takes her, and he lays with her. End of story.

But as it turns out, that is not the end of the story. Of all the inconvenient things, Bathsheba, the object of King David's lust, finds herself pregnant after their encounter, and she sends word to David. Once an object of lust, Bathsheba now becomes another "object," in the form of a problem to be solved.

COVER UPS AND LIES

In order to hide his wrongdoing, David sends for Bathsheba's husband, Uriah the Hittite, who is away at war. Knowing Uriah would be surprised to find his wife pregnant when he has not been with her, David tells Uriah to spend some time at home. He hopes that Uriah will have sex with his wife and then will believe the child Bathsheba carries is his own.

But Uriah, an apparently honorable man who is loyal to God, his king, and his fellow warriors, does not return home, and messes up David's royal plan:

> But Uriah slept at the door of the king's house with all the servants of his lord, and did not go down to his house. When they told David, "Uriah did not go down to his house," David said to Uriah, "Have you not come from a journey? Why did you not go down to your house?" Uriah said to David, "The ark and Israel and Judah dwell in booths; and my lord Joab and the servants of my lord are camping in the open field; shall I then go to my house, to eat and to drink, and to lie with my wife? As you live, and as your soul lives, I will not do this thing" (2 Samuel 11:9-11).

David tries again to make Uriah go home to Bathsheba, even getting him drunk in the hopes that he will stagger home, but none of it works. In the end, David decides he has no choice but to murder Uriah in order to cover up his sin.

He sends Uriah back to battle, delivering a message to Joab. The message, delivered by Uriah's own hand, tells Joab to set up Uriah in the forefront of the hardest fighting and then to pull back so that Uriah will be killed. Joab does as he is told, and Uriah is killed in battle.

And so it is that David uses Bathsheba as an object of his lust and then deprives her of her husband, by all accounts a good and loyal man, when she has the audacity to wind up pregnant. And so it is that Bathsheba suffers again.

> When the wife of Uriah heard that Uriah her husband was dead, she made lamentation for her husband. And when the mourning was over, David sent and brought her to his house, and she became his wife, and bore him a son (2 Samuel 11:26-27).

All wrapped up neatly, right? No one sees, and no one has to know what injustice Bathsheba has suffered at the hands of a selfish king.

Not so fast, though. The very next line in the Bible story tells us something important. The very next line tells us that someone does see. God sees, God knows, and Bathsheba matters:

"But the thing that David had done displeased the LORD" (2 Samuel 11:27).

ONE LITTLE EWE LAMB

Next, God sends the prophet Nathan to David to tell him a dramatic story. The story is about a poor man who has nothing in the world but "one little ewe lamb" that is precious to him.

"And he brought it up, and it grew up with him and with his children; it used to eat of his morsel, and drink from his cup, and lie in his bosom, and it was like a daughter to him" (2 Samuel 12:3).

The story goes on to tell about a rich man, who has many flocks and herds. When this rich man receives a visitor, however, instead of choosing one of his own animals to eat, he takes and kills the one little ewe lamb that belongs to the poor man.

Upon hearing this story, King David grows very angry and says, "As the LORD lives, the man who has done this deserves to die" (2 Samuel 12:5).

Imagine his surprise when Nathan replies:

> You are the man. Thus says the LORD, the God of Israel, "I anointed you king over Israel, and I delivered you out of the hand of Saul; and I gave you your master's house, and your master's wives into your bosom, and gave you the house of Israel and of Judah; and if this were too little, I would add to you as much more. Why have you despised the word of the LORD, to do what is evil in his sight? You have struck down Uriah the Hittite with the sword, and have taken his wife to be your wife, and have slain him with the sword of the Ammonites" (2 Samuel 12:7-9).

God knows all. He sees all. He knows the injustice that has been done to Uriah and also the injustice that has been done to Bathsheba. It is fitting that in Nathan's story, Bathsheba is represented as a precious little ewe lamb that is "like a daughter" to the poor man. Later, in the New Testament, we often hear Jesus refer to himself as a loving shepherd and to each of us as his precious lambs, the ones for whom he lays down his life. Bathsheba is just that to God—a precious lamb, his precious daughter—and he speaks that truth through the words of Nathan, the prophet.

You are that precious lamb, too. Just like God saw and knew Bathsheba in her hidden pain, he sees you and knows you in yours. Your suffering, even when hidden from the eyes of others, is recognized by God the Father. It matters, and so do you.

CONSEQUENCES OF SIN

Very often, in cases of sexual sin, women are the ones who suffer the most. Inside a sexual relationship, women, because they can become pregnant, are more vulnerable than men. Also, because women are more naturally focused on relationships and bonding, especially through sex and motherhood, we are left even further vulnerable to the consequences of sexual sin. Quite simply, we have more to lose.

This is certainly true for Bathsheba. Because of her pregnancy, she not only loses her husband, Uriah, but she also loses the son she eventually gives birth to. Nathan explains that this loss is part of God's punishment for David's sin:

> "Nevertheless, because by this deed you have utterly scorned the LORD, the child that is born to you shall die" ... And the LORD struck the child that Uriah's wife bore to David, and it became sick ... On the seventh day the child died (2 Samuel 12:14-18).

Because of David's sin, Bathsheba suffers the loss of her child. Similarly, in today's world, many women find themselves facing the crisis of an unplanned pregnancy alone, despite the fact that it "took two to tango." Many women suffer the burden of single parenthood as a result of sexual sin, and many others suffer before, during, and after choosing abortion in the face of an unplanned pregnancy.

Abortion hurts women especially, as it attacks us at the core of our motherhood. It destroys the loving bond that every one of us knows in our heart is meant to exist between a mother and her child, the very motherhood we intuitively know we are meant to fulfill as part of our calling as women.

You or someone you know might have suffered or might be suffering as a result of choosing abortion. God sees this pain, too. It is a great injustice of our times that any woman would ever feel desperate and alone enough to end her child's life within her. A culture that leaves any woman feeling like abortion is her best option when facing an unplanned pregnancy is a culture that has devalued women, abandoned them, and left them alone to carry a burden that was meant to be shared. Despite her innocence, Bathsheba bore the burdensome consequences of sexual sin, just as many of us—both innocent and complicit—do in today's world. God sees this pain and this injustice too.

LOVED AT LAST

This is not the end of Bathsheba's story. While their relationship certainly does not begin with mutual love, respect, and understanding, Bathsheba and David's relationship seems to grow into something more meaningful and loving after the death of their child:

"Then David comforted his wife, Bathsheba, and went in to her, and lay with her; and she bore a son, and he called his name Solomon. And the LORD loved him" (2 Samuel 12:24).

The fact that David publicly repents of his sin, and that Bathsheba then allows David to comfort her tells us that their relationship is growing in mercy and love. Bathsheba's son Solomon goes on to become successor to David and a great king, thus making her the Queen Mother and earning her an honored place in the genealogy of Jesus.

We read the genealogy of Jesus in the New Testament of the Bible in the first chapter of Matthew, where Bathsheba, one of only four women included, is listed as the mother of Solomon, but not by name. She is referred to as "the wife of Uriah" (Matthew 1:6).

This small detail matters because the words of the Bible, which are God's words, contain no accidents. Bathsheba is referred to as the "wife of Uriah" because God knows that is her rightful identity and that it has been taken from her. Though David's sin gives Bathsheba the opportunity to become a part of the lineage of Jesus, God sees who she was, who she is, and what she has suffered. He sees these things and leaves them, spelled out plainly for all to read and know, for generations to come.

TAMAR, BETRAYED BY HER BROTHER

In the very next chapter of the second book of Samuel, we meet another of our ancient sisters who suffers greatly because of the actions and betrayals of bad men in her life.

Tamar is one of King David's daughters, the sister of Absalom. As such, she is a princess and likely has a high-status marriage planned, one that would have been arranged when she was very young.

Tamar is very beautiful, the Bible tells us, and her half-brother Amnon falls in love with her. Well, the passage says he "loved" her, but truth be told, the descriptions that follow sound more like an unhealthy obsession:

"Amnon was so tormented that he made himself ill because of his sister Tamar; for she was a virgin, and it seemed impossible to Amnon to do anything to her" (2 Samuel 13:2).

He is sick because he cannot "do anything to her"? Does this sound like love to you?

In ancient Israel, half siblings were sometimes permitted to marry, though it was typically discouraged. Amnon does not appear to consider this a possibility, however, as Tamar has likely been promised to someone else. Instead, he and a deceitful friend come up with an evil plan.

Amnon lies down and pretends to be ill. When his father, King David, becomes concerned and goes to him, he asks David to send his sister Tamar to prepare food for him and feed him from her own hand in order to make him well. David summons Tamar immediately, and she goes to care for her brother. She prepares cakes for Amnon, but at first, he refuses to eat them. He then sends all the servants out and asks Tamar to bring the food into his private chamber and feed it to him by hand. This is when he assaults her.

> But when she brought them near him to eat, he took hold of her, and said to her, "Come lie with me, my sister." She answered him, "No, my brother, do not force me; for such a thing is not done in Israel; do not do this wanton folly. As for me, where could I carry my shame? And as for you, you would be as one of the wanton fools in Israel. Now therefore, I beg you, speak to the king; for he will not withhold me from you" (2 Samuel 13:11-13).

Amnon will not listen to reason, however, and he rapes Tamar. "Being stronger than she, he forced her, and lay with her" (2 Samuel 13:14).

He is stronger. He forces her. He lays with her. Any woman who has ever been a victim of sexual assault knows the kind of devastating violation these plain words describe.

Unlike what we read in the story of David and Bathsheba, however, what follows this terrible sin against an innocent woman is not a story of repentance, healing, and love. What follows is hatred and rejection. Immediately after the rape, Amnon's "love" for his sister becomes feelings of guilt and shame that take the form of hatred against her.

> Then Amnon hated her with a very great hatred; so that the hatred with which he hated her was greater than the love with which he had loved her. And Amnon said to her, "Arise, be gone" (2 Samuel 13:15).

Now that she is no longer a virgin, Tamar knows that the entirety of her once-bright future has been taken from her. She pleads with Amnon to let her stay, so she can salvage her reputation and they can make things right.

> But she said to him, "No, my brother; for this wrong in sending me away is greater than the other which you did to me." But he would not listen to her. He called the young man who served him and said, "Put this woman out of my presence, and bolt the door after her" (2 Samuel 13:16-17).

MORE BETRAYAL

Raped by her brother and thrown out of his home, Tamar decides not to try to hide her brother's crime and very publicly announces what has happened instead. She puts ashes on her head, rends her garment, lays her hand on her head, and goes out wailing—all of which were typical demonstrations of mourning in the culture at the time.

She goes and tells all to her brother Absalom, who takes her into his home. He is angry at his brother for what he has done, and when King David learns of it, he is angry, too. Yet no one seems quite angry enough to take any immediate action against Amnon. He remains unpunished.

Tamar, however, is severely punished for having been raped. She can no longer marry the noble man she has been promised to. She no longer can wear the fancy robes high-status virgins wear and enjoy the respect and admiration of others. She must spend her days in lonely isolation, suffering the shame of her brother's crime against her.

If you have ever been a victim of rape or sexual assault, you might know a little bit about the kind of desolation Tamar felt in those days, weeks, months, and years following her brother's crime. In looking at the details of this disturbing story, we see that Tamar was betrayed, not just by her brother Amnon, who attacked her, but also by her father, her other brother, and by a culture that made her pay the price for her brother's wrongdoing.

As her father, King David should have protected Tamar. He should have listened to his instincts, which would have told him Amnon's request to be hand-fed by his sister, alone in his home, was a suspicious one. He should have known his son's weakness and done all he could to keep Tamar far away from the risky situation he placed her in. Finally, after he learned of Amnon's violent act against Tamar, he should have punished Amnon and publicly denounced what he had done.

We read only that, "When King David heard of all these things, he was very angry" (2 Samuel 13:21).

A lot of good that anger does for Tamar while she suffers social rejection and hides in shame at her other brother's house.

Similarly, Tamar's brother Absalom, though very angry about the rape, also takes no immediate action against his brother. Instead, we read that he bides his time and lets his hatred for his brother fester for two years. After two years, he at last orders his men to kill Amnon, ostensibly as revenge for what was done to Tamar, but it also happens to be a politically expedient thing for Absalom to do, as this move benefits his own ambition to gain his father's throne over his brother.

A lot of good Absalom's revenge does for Tamar when she is still subjected to a life of shame and hiding.

TELLING HER STORY

In reading Tamar's story, every woman who has ever felt violated or betrayed by a man who was supposed to protect her can find solace in the fact that this story has been written and given the status it has as a part of the Bible.

Amnon raped Tamar, David failed to protect her, Absalom used her victimhood for political gain, and her own people rejected her, but God saw Tamar in her desolation, and he affirmed her dignity by allowing her story to be told. He saw the injustices perpetrated against Tamar and allowed their details to be written down and included in his own book, the Bible.

God saw Tamar and knew her worth, even when no one else around her did, and that is why we can open the Bible and read her story today. Tamar might not have had much power to seek justice during the time in which she lived, but her story remains, and it has the power to reach every woman today with a message of God's affirmation and love.

Some cultures and religions today still enforce laws that punish women who are the victims of rape. Under Sharia law in Saudi Arabia, for example, a victim of rape sometimes receives an even harsher sentence than her rapist. Systems that so blatantly reject the dignity and worth of women are an obvious example of injustice, but there are subtler forms in our own culture as well.

Victims of rape, even in "enlightened" cultures like ours, often suffer an unjust burden of guilt and shame for what happened to them. What's more, their stories are sometimes not believed, and rape victims themselves are sometimes subjected to cruel questioning, suspected of being complicit in their attacks, and asked what they might have done to entice their attackers.

Are you the victim of injustice? Have you ever been? Do you carry the wounds of someone who betrayed you or violated your dignity in the past? Whatever kind of injustice or betrayal we might experience or witness, especially those unjust things that might happen to us because we are women, we can remember the story of Tamar and know that God sees the injustice against us and speaks the truth about its evil.

Just as God saw Tamar and knew what had been done to her, God sees you and knows the wrongs that have been done to you. Even when others failed to listen and see, God knew that Tamar's story was important. It was so important that he allowed it to be described, in detail, in the Bible for all future generations to hear. Tamar's story in the Bible is not nuanced. It is the ugly truth, told plainly. It confirms that Tamar was a virtuous woman, victimized by the actions and failures of the men who were supposed to love her and care for her. It illustrates the importance of her experience and her worth as a daughter of God.

Through the tragic story of Tamar and its inclusion in the Bible, God affirms that your story matters, too. Like Bathsheba and Tamar, you, too, are a precious daughter of God. He sees you in your suffering, and your experience matters. God wants to give you a voice; he wants to give your story the hearing it deserves. He wants to lift you up.

What is your story? Are you suffering? What do you want to say? What truths will you speak about the injustice that has been done to you and to other women?

Let's start talking. Let's speak out. Let's begin.

CLOSING PRAYER

Our Father, you would not willingly call on us to suffer. You say all things work together for our good if we are faithful to you. Therefore, if you ordain it: through disappointment and poverty, sickness and pain, even shame and contempt and calumny, you will support us with the consolation of your Grace and compensate us for any temporal suffering by the possession of that peace which the world can neither give nor take away.

St. Elizabeth Ann Seton

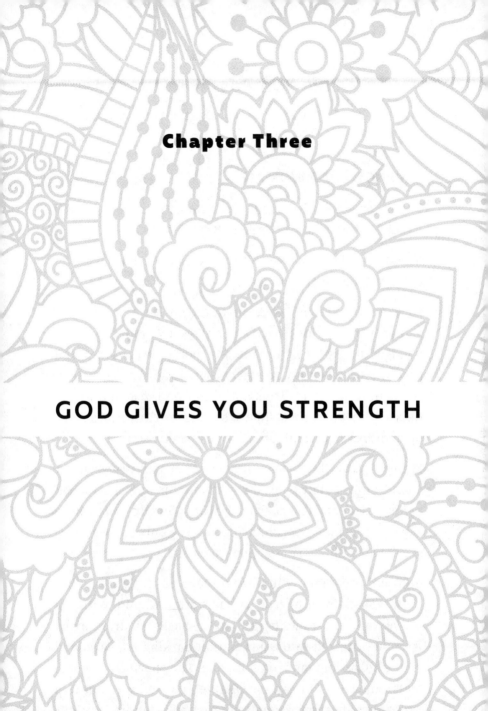

Chapter Three

GOD GIVES YOU STRENGTH

God Gives You Power to Do Great Things and the Freedom to Choose

STRENGTH OF A WOMAN

I don't remember the details of the car accident so much as I recall my mother's shaky relief after the fact.

"Thank God, thank God you all are OK," she repeated over and over, hugging each of us close.

I was four years old, traveling in the backseat of our 1972 station wagon with two of my sisters, one older and one younger, on either side of me. My mother was in the front seat driving, when my younger sister, Susie, who was about two at the time, decided that now would be a good time to free herself from her car seat (they were less restrictive back then), open the car door, and tumble onto the busy street below.

My mother saw this in her rearview mirror, and as any mother would, immediately panicked. Without thinking, she opened her own door and leaped from the car to pick up Susie before she could be hit by oncoming traffic. The only problem was, she did not fully stop the station wagon and put it in park first.

And so it was that my mother rescued our little sister, but then looked on in horror as our station wagon, with my six-year-old sister and me still in the backseat, drove away from her, turned into a gas station parking lot, careened over a ledge, and landed on its side. The enormous vehicle teetered back and forth for what felt like minutes but was probably only a few seconds before finally landing upright, wheels on the ground, stopped.

Suddenly, we were surrounded by people pulling my sister and me from the car and looking us over to see that we were OK. I was confused because among the people present was our mailman, Mr. Rolerad, whom I never saw except when he was on his route in our neighborhood. Apparently, Mr. Rolerad had been pumping gas when our driverless car made its way past him, and he witnessed the whole horrifying scene.

I recall the fear of seeing the world turn sideways through the car window, but for the most part, I was too young to fully grasp what happened that day. My mother's response, though, told me it was something serious.

She led us all in a prayer of thanksgiving for our safety and then said weakly, "I thought you were all gone. Your guardian angels must have been here, pushing the car in the right direction."

The following day, when Mr. Rolerad delivered our mail, he stopped in to check on my mom and the rest of us. When he asked my mother how she was feeling, she answered, "I'm OK, but I am so sore all over, and I cannot figure out why. My back and shoulders are really aching."

"Well, I know why," Mr. Rolerad replied immediately. "It's because yesterday you tried to stop a moving vehicle with nothing but your own two hands."

Then our mailman went on to describe how my mom rescued Susie from the road and then raced after our moving car. My mother, barely over five feet tall and barely over one hundred pounds, grabbed hold of the moving station wagon and attempted to stop it with her own strength. Failing at this, she leaped over the ledge after the car, and was standing next to the giant mass of metal as it teetered back and forth. Had the car landed on its roof, as all who watched feared it might, my mother would have been crushed beneath it.

My mom remembered none of this.

WONDER WOMEN

Sometimes, we don't know our own strength until we are challenged, and for many of us, motherhood brings out a strength in us that we did not previously know existed. Under different circumstances, my mom would never have considered trying to manhandle a moving vehicle, but when her daughters were inside and in immediate danger, she fearlessly leaped into action. A real-life Wonder Woman.

We love Wonder Woman, don't we? In the popular 2017 film *Wonder Woman*, the main character, Diana Prince, is admirable not only for her strength but also for her beauty, courage, compassion, and wisdom. Even those of us who never stop moving trains with our own bare hands or run recklessly through battlefields, deflecting bullets and dodging landmines, love stories of superheroes like Wonder Woman. We love these stories because they call attention to gifts of womanly strength we recognize as real, even if the superheroes are not.

Have you ever felt uniquely powerful as a woman? Not in spite of being a woman, but *because you are a woman?*

I was first surprised by my own womanly strength early in my motherhood, when I gave birth for the first time. As is the case for many new moms, not all went as I thought it would. I was blessed to have an uncomplicated labor and delivery, but the entire birth scenario involved significantly less meditation accompanied by the sounds of Celtic monks chanting in a rainforest and significantly more expulsion of various bodily fluids than I originally anticipated.

Nevertheless, I battled through waves of pain and seas of uncertainty, and in the end, I delivered a healthy baby girl that the nurses bundled and placed on my chest.

I was awestruck. Not only by the tiny blinking miracle that I held, but also by my own strength—physical, emotional, and spiritual—that had gotten me through the ordeal.

Where did that come from?

I felt I had discovered a deep truth about myself through that first birth experience. I was a woman, and as such, I was made strong. Specifically, I was made strong for the unique, womanly tasks that God called me to. Not only in my motherhood but in all the ways God was calling me to serve others in my life. Quite simply, I was made for this.

I was never one to use corny words like "empowering" before, but that was the best word to use to describe how I felt I was changed by giving birth. The experience empowered me as a woman and as a mom. I, the introverted girl who was allergic to conflict and who thanked police officers for traffic tickets, felt powerful. Maybe for the first time in my life.

You might never have chased a runaway car or given birth, but every woman can know this much: God has gifted you with unique womanly strength that he calls you to use in service to others—perhaps as a mom or as a sister, teacher, aunt, co-worker, or neighbor. You know the circumstances God has placed you in, and therefore, you know the details of the ways in which God gives you strength to answer his call.

SURPRISED BY STRENGTH

Have you ever felt surprised by your own courage or strength? Perhaps you felt inspired to stand up in the face of injustice, to speak out in defense of someone more vulnerable than you, or even to place yourself in harm's way in order to protect someone else, whether it was your own child or a complete stranger.

Part of the source of our courage in situations like these is the unique capacity women have for sensitivity to others and intuitive understanding of relationships and connections. These gifts make us different from men, and they come from God. In addition, God gives us gifts of beauty, generosity, and a unique capacity for self-giving, nurturing love. From the beginning of time, human beings have shared stories that highlight feminine gifts like these.

Of course, these strengths present themselves differently in every woman, but we all share uniquely feminine strengths in common. God means for us to use our womanly gifts and strengths to love and care for the people he places in our lives, but it is our choice to do so.

The reality of feminine strength in all its various forms is an important enough universal truth that it is highlighted in some of the most powerful stories of the Bible. Just as we can learn about the ways in which God sees and cares for each of us individually through the stories of women in the Old Testament, we can also discover the timelessness of womanly strength and the ways in which God calls each of us to use our own unique version of it from stories of women in the Bible.

One of the most memorable and powerful women we read about in the Bible is Judith. Judith's story is so important that she has her own book in the Bible all to herself! In the book of Judith, we read about how this holy and wise widow defeats an enemy general and saves God's people from imminent destruction. The details of Judith's triumph over the enemy are surprising, dramatic, and astonishing. She defeats the enemy general by gaining his trust, tricking him, and then, when he least suspects it, beheading him with his own sword.

You read that right. She cut off a man's head. Here we have the female version of David and Goliath, but King David can keep his slain giant. Judith has the head of Holofernes. Let's read on to find out how this came to be.

JUDITH, RIGHTEOUS DAUGHTER OF GOD

The first several chapters of the book of Judith are devoted to describing the strength of the enemies of the Israelite people in a small town called Bethulia. A powerful Assyrian army, under the leadership of General Holofernes, has conquered all surrounding areas, and now the Israelites look like easy prey for their approaching enemy.

It is only in Judith 8, after reading pages describing the people's hopelessness and suffering, that we finally meet Judith. Judith is a wealthy widow in the city of Bethulia, whose late husband has left her with status—some property, wealth, and servants.

Judith is beautiful, but also a holy and righteous woman who respects and obeys God:

> She was beautiful in appearance, and had a very lovely face ... Her husband Manasseh ... had left her gold and silver, and men and women slaves, and cattle, and fields; and she maintained this estate. No one spoke ill of her, for she feared God with great devotion (Judith 8:7-8).

Upon learning that the leaders of her small city are planning to surrender under the impending attack by their enemy in

five days, Judith calls upon her leaders and chastises them for
their lack of faith in God:

> No, my brethren, do not provoke the Lord our God to anger.
> For if he does not choose to help us within these five days,
> he has power to protect us within any time he pleases, or
> even to destroy us in the presence of our enemies. Do not
> try to bind the purposes of the Lord our God; for God is
> not like man, to be threatened, nor like a human being, to
> be won over by pleading. Therefore, while we wait for his
> deliverance, let us call upon him to help us, and he will hear
> our voice, if it pleases him (Judith 8:14-17).

Judith's words here convey a deep sense of trust in God's
goodness, as well as great respect for his almighty power
to save her people. Judith understands that God's ways are
different from man's ways, and she trusts that God will save
her people from their enemies. The male leaders of Bethulia
are lacking in understanding in all these areas of faith.

BEGUILED BY BEAUTY

After demonstrating her strength of righteousness and faith,
Judith next employs her feminine gift of beauty in service to
God. We need look no further than the greatest works of art
in the history of mankind to know that there is something
uniquely beautiful about women's faces and bodies. Our
modern world gets feminine beauty wrong in many ways and
often uses female beauty to turn women into sexual objects
to be used by men for lustful purposes—or even just to sell
razor blades—but our secular society certainly recognizes the
unique allure of feminine beauty.

Woman is the apex of God's creation. We may not all be supermodels, but every woman is made with a natural sense of beauty, which is different from a man's, and God created every woman's body to be a physical expression of real beauty—a kind of beauty which is meant to be a reflection of God and therefore give glory to him.

Judith recognizes that she has the power of beauty, and she does not hesitate to use it as part of her plan to defeat the enemies of her people. She even emphasizes it, in fact, so as to gain an advantage over the men she wants to control. Before she begins, however, she makes clear that everything she is about to do is in service to God by first falling down in prayer and asking for God's help in her work.

> Behold their pride, and send your wrath upon their heads; give to me, a widow, the strength to do what I plan. By the deceit of my lips strike down the slave with the prince and the prince with his servant; crush their arrogance by the hand of a woman (Judith 9:9-10).

Note that Judith does not take pride in her gifts, and she does not seek to glorify herself through them, but she asks only for God's help in using her gifts to save her people. After steeping her actions in prayer this way, she makes herself ready.

She removes her sackcloth, takes off her widow's garments, and bathes herself. After bathing, she anoints herself with precious ointment, combs her hair, and puts on a tiara. A tiara! Obviously, Judith is going all out, but that's not all ...

> And she put sandals on her feet, and put on her anklets and bracelets and rings, and her earrings and all her ornaments, and made herself very beautiful, to entice the eyes of all men who might see her (Judith 10:4).

All this "bling," meant to highlight her natural beauty, does the trick. She readily gains permission from Uzziah, the leader of her people, to open the city gates and sets out with her maid in order to infiltrate and overthrow their Assyrian enemies.

Almost immediately, the two women are met by an Assyrian patrol who take them into custody. She tells these men that she wants to speak to their leader, Holofernes, and tell him a way that he can defeat her own people. Overcome by her beauty, the men accede to her request.

> When the men heard her words, and observed her face—she was in their eyes marvelously beautiful—they said to her, "You have saved your life by hurrying down to the presence of our lord. Go at once to his tent; some of us will escort you and hand you over to him" (Judith 10:14-15).

Supermodels or not, most women know the kind of power their feminine beauty can have over men, and many of us have used it. Have we always used it in service to God and his people? Maybe not. Later in this chapter, we will read more about another woman in the Bible who misuses her attractiveness to exploit a man and achieve selfish desires.

God gives all women powerful gifts like our physical beauty, but he also gives us the gift of freedom. God allows each of us to choose whether to use our gifts for good or for evil. Judith chooses to serve God not only with her beauty, but also with her wisdom and courage. Let's continue with her story.

STRENGTH OF WISDOM

When Judith meets with Holofernes, he, too, is quite taken with her beauty. It seems that all Judith needs to do is smile and men fall down at her feet. She also uses her wisdom and insight to gain the confidence of Holofernes as well. Knowing his ego, she presents a long-winded, descriptive speech, using words and ideas that flatter the general.

> Her words pleased Holofernes and all his servants, and they marveled at her wisdom and said, "There is not such a woman from one end of the earth to the other, either for beauty of face or wisdom of speech!" (Judith 11:20-21).

Holofernes orders that Judith be brought into one of his tents, where she stays for three days, praying each night and eating her own food and drinking her own drink. On the fourth day, Holofernes invites Judith to a special banquet, and she accepts.

While they are together, eating and drinking, Holofernes is so pleased with Judith's company and beauty and so enthralled at the prospect of sleeping with her, that he drinks way too much wine. In fact, "much more than he had ever drunk in any one day since he was born" (Judith 12:20).

The general's servants leave Judith alone with Holofernes, who is passed out drunk, presuming that the two will sleep together, and so it is that Judith's plan has come to fruition, and the time has come for her to act.

STRENGTH OF COURAGE

Can you even imagine what you would think and feel in a moment like this one? We may not all have opportunities to behead enemy generals, but we all do have times in our lives when we need the courage to do what needs to be done.

It takes courage to decide to leave a bad relationship. It takes courage to stand up to medical or educational professionals and demand what is best for our children. It takes courage to speak the truth when someone has hurt us. It takes courage to speak out against wrongdoing at work, especially when we know that our co-workers may not understand and may not support us.

In every moment where we are called to do something that takes courage, we can look to Judith's example of acting when called to do so. Judith does not act out of fear or revenge. She does not recklessly attack Holofernes. She recognizes the importance of the action she is being called to take in defense of God's people, and she pauses to pray before taking it.

> Judith, standing beside his bed, said in her heart, "O Lord God of all might, look in this hour upon the work of my hands for the exaltation of Jerusalem. For now is the time to help your inheritance, and to carry out my undertaking for the destruction of the enemies who have risen up against us" (Judith 13:4-5).

Judith recognizes that God is the source of every gift and strength that she has used to bring her to this moment, and so before taking any action, she asks God for his help and reminds herself of the noble reasons she has for doing it. Only then does she take Holofernes' sword and cut off his head. She gives the head to her maid who places it in her food bag. Then the two women race home and call for the men to open the gates to Bethulia and let them in. News that Holofernes has been slain spreads quickly, and there is great rejoicing in the city.

Of course, Judith's story is a wild one to modern ears. So few, if any, of us will ever face a situation where we are called upon to slay an enemy general during a time of war, and yet there are evils we are called upon to overcome.

What evils do you see in the world, in your community, or even in your own home that God might be calling you to overcome? Do you know that God gives you the gifts and strengths that are exactly what you need to accomplish whatever he is calling you to do? Even simple things like speaking the truth and defending vulnerable people can take a great deal of courage and conviction sometimes.

God is the source of every gift and strength you have, and he calls you to use these gifts in service to the people he places in your life. In what ways might God be calling you to use your gifts of beauty, intuition, wisdom, or courage to do good things in the world? In what ways can you, like Judith, turn to God for strength and take courageous action?

STRENGTH MISUSED

God gives each of us gifts, and he gives uniquely feminine gifts to every woman, but he also gives us the gift of freedom. He allows us to choose how we will use the good things he gives us. We have already mentioned the ways in which the world sometimes misuses the gift of feminine beauty and the ways in which women might be tempted to use their beauty for selfish gain, to build up their own egos, or to manipulate men for bad purposes.

In fact, there are examples of women in the Old Testament who use their gifts of intuition, beauty, and wit for evil purposes. Perhaps the most famous of these is Delilah, Samson's lover.

Samson is a man of great strength whom we meet in the book of Judges. He has been consecrated to God from his birth and has defeated and killed many Philistines. As such, the Philistines are keenly interested in learning the source of his strength (we know that it is his hair) so that they can defeat him.

Samson is a physically strong man, but a morally weak one. We read about the many women with whom he has sexual affairs, and he even has a wife for a time whom he mistreats and then abandons. But there is one woman he says he "loves," and that woman is Delilah.

Delilah does not love Samson, but she is willing to use his infatuation with her for her own gain. She is a Philistine, and therefore, Samson is the enemy of her people. The Philistines offer Delilah a great sum of money if she can find out the source of Samson's strength so that they might defeat him.

Motivated by greed, Delilah seduces Samson over the course of several days, begging him to prove his love for her by telling her the secret of his strength. At first, Samson puts her off by telling her false things like that he will lose his strength if he is tied up with fresh ropes. Each time, Delilah tests what he tells her and calls for the Philistines to come take him away. Each time, however, Samson breaks free, as strong as ever, and the Philistines fail in their attempt to take him.

Samson really is a pathetic character here when at last Delilah succeeds in getting him to trust her with the real secret—that if his head is shaved, he will lose his strength. She lulls him to sleep on her lap, and then calls a man to shave his head. Samson becomes as weak as any other man, and Delilah turns him over to the Philistines who gouge out his eyes and throw him into prison.

Why on earth would Samson trust Delilah with the truth when every other time he has tested her, she has attempted to turn him over to his enemy? We are left to believe that he is so blinded by his "love" for her and his desire to please her that he is powerless to withhold the truth.

A man's desire to please a woman he loves is indeed a powerful thing, and it can be a great motivator to men to rise to higher standards. But Delilah misuses her sexual power over Samson for her own greedy goals. She manipulates him and uses her beauty to seduce him in exchange for payment. Of course, this is not what God had in mind when he blessed Delilah with her beauty.

Just like the women we meet in the Bible, every woman today also has powerful gifts, given to her by God, and the freedom to choose how to use them.

What feminine strengths has God given you? The power of beauty, the strength of courage, the gift of intuition and sensitivity to others? Are there ways in which you are sometimes tempted to use these gifts in selfish ways? In what ways might God be calling you to use your gifts and abilities to serve the people he has placed in your life—your family, your friends, your co-workers, and the world at large?

The remarkable story of a heroine like Judith and its inclusion in the Bible underscores the truth that God gives every woman gifts of strength. The memorable story of a selfish woman like Delilah, however, demonstrates the fact that each of us is also given the freedom to choose how we will use our strengths. We can use gifts of beauty, courage, wisdom, and intuition to use other people for our own selfish gains, or we can choose to use them in service to God by blessing the people he places in our lives.

We can be inspired by stories we read in the Bible, but of course, we don't need to seduce weak-willed men or slay enemy generals to embrace the womanly strength God gives us. Open your heart now to hear the ways in which God gives you unique strength and how he wants you to use that strength to do his work, to love and care for others. Take courage as you step into whatever role he calls you to.

CLOSING PRAYER

Christ has no body now on earth but yours;
no hands but yours; no feet but yours. Yours are
the eyes through which the compassion of Christ
must look out on the world. Yours are the feet
with which he is to go about doing good. Yours are
the hands with which he is to bless his people.

St. Teresa of Avila

Chapter Four

GOD GIVES YOU HOPE

God Knows the Desires of Your Heart, and They Are Good

PREGNANT AND PINING

I heaved my aching body onto the couch and propped my swollen feet on the coffee table, sighing loudly. My husband, Dan, sat down next to me and asked if anything was wrong.

"Oh, nothing," I lied.

After a long routine of bedtime stories, brushing teeth, glasses of water, and stuffed animal emergencies, we had just gotten our three young children settled into their beds for the night. I was weeks away from my due date with our fourth baby in almost as many years, and truth be told, I was exhausted—not just from the physical stress of the pregnancy and caring for a young family, but mentally exhausted as well.

We were quickly outgrowing the small home we were renting and were in the process of building a house of our own. Despite my belief that "normal" people buy houses that are already built and ready to move into, Dan had convinced me that it made sense to invest all our savings in the purchase of a piece of land and a down payment on a construction loan to build a place of our own in the country.

The problem was that now we were beginning to make payments on that loan, in addition to our monthly rent, and the house we were building was far from move-in ready. In fact, it was only a cleared piece of land, a well, a septic system, and a poured foundation so far. This was early in my career as wife to a do-it-yourself, building kind of husband, and I was just beginning to figure out that construction projects generally take about twice as long as you think they will going into them.

With Dan's salary as a teacher in a small Catholic school as our only income, our budget was tight—so tight that it kept me awake many nights just wondering how we could make it all work.

I did what I could to save money. I made many of our foods from scratch to save on groceries and shopped at thrift stores for the kids' clothes. Dan helped out in every way he could, too. He even took on a second job, working late nights loading trucks for UPS. Truly, though, if we were going to make any progress on our new house, we needed him to spend more time focused on the building project, and its completion seemed like a long time away.

Toward the end of that pregnancy, I spent my more challenging days thinking about those tricky words in our wedding vows. For richer and for poorer. Funny how on that glorious summer day when we said those words, meaning what we said felt easy. Our entire future looked only richer, and we had no idea of the kinds of struggles that lay ahead.

The worst part of that "poorer" time in our family life was that it wasn't just a house I wanted. I also wanted a car—specifically, a minivan. Our ancient Volvo station wagon had served us well for many years, but it was becoming less and less reliable, and it would be a real trick to squeeze four car seats in the back. Dan drove an even smaller Toyota, and so once the new baby arrived, we would not have a vehicle we could comfortably fit our entire family in.

If you have ever been pregnant, you probably know a bit about the ways in which hormones can affect your moods and thoughts. For me, especially late in pregnancy, I become hyper focused on preparing our physical spaces for the new baby. With our house, our car, and our budget feeling inadequate in the weeks leading up to the new baby's birth, I might have become just a little bit difficult to live with.

"I just want to be *normal*," I whined to Dan one day when we were talking about the car situation.

"Normal?" he challenged me gently. "What is normal? Most people in the world don't own one car, never mind two they don't think fit their needs."

Oh, I see. He was going to play the first world privilege card with me. After that conversation, I decided not to pressure Dan any more with my impossible desire for a new car, but still the longing remained.

Desperate, I brought my longing to God instead. I would like to say that I prayed for a new car in an inspiring, beautifully faithful, and hopeful way, but that would be a lie. Truth be told, I prayed for a new car in a bratty way. The entire time I prayed, I thought that what I was asking God for was perfectly impossible, even for him, and that he was probably annoyed at my petty request.

But the habits formed in me as a cradle Catholic pushed me to persevere. I asked God to somehow help us get a new car. I prayed to the saints. I prayed novenas. I silently added the intention to our family's grace as we prayed before meals. And all the time I prayed, I mentally rolled my eyes at the very idea that, with absolutely no wiggle room in our super-tight budget, it would be even remotely possible for us to get a new car before the baby was born. This just wasn't going to happen.

I didn't tell Dan what I was praying for, and he was too focused on work and completing our house to notice anyway.

The baby was due any day now, and I was getting through my days in that kind of panicked mode a pregnant mom gets into when the baby's arrival seems imminent and the waiting keeps her on edge. If there were any surprises or sudden sounds, I would think, *Oh, it's the baby!* I was that anxious.

So, I startled when the phone rang in the late afternoon on one of those days, but it wasn't the baby. It was Dan, saying he would be home in about an hour, and he had a surprise for me. I tried to tell him that a surprise was the last thing my pregnant nerves needed, but he only said he would see me soon and hung up the phone.

An hour later, Dan pulled into our driveway in a light brown minivan. He stepped out of the van and smiled at my confusion.

"Whose car is this?" I asked.

"It's ours!" he laughed, jingling the keys in my direction.

"What? How?"

The minivan belonged to the priests at the school where he taught, Dan explained, and though it still worked well, they were replacing it with a new one. And so they were giving us the old one. *Giving it to us.*

"They just came and offered it to me," Dan said. "I don't know why they thought of us."

I sat my pregnant self down in the grass, and I cried.

GOD LISTENS AND CARES

I was humbled by that experience of God listening to and responding to my imperfect trust and my doubt-filled prayers. It's embarrassing to admit that it took a free minivan to make it happen, but for perhaps the first time in my life, God's love felt personal and real to me.

God was not a gumball machine in the sky where we put our prayers in and turn the handle to collect our prize. God was a loving Father, listening to and caring about the desires of my weak and human heart. God wanted a relationship with me. He was calling me to draw closer to him through my desires and the prayers they prompted me to say. He was teaching me who he was and helping me to know that he wanted good things for me.

He wants good things for you, too.

What is it that you want most? Health and safety for yourself and your family? Financial security? Love and peace in your home? Or maybe just a new minivan?

It's OK to admit that some of our longings are trivial in comparison to the needs of others. God sees all your desires, the big ones and the small ones. Some of the most basic desires we have as women, God put there himself. He made us to long for love, peace, happiness, and security so that we might learn to seek him out as the source of all good things. He hears even our imperfect prayers for even very small things, and he works with our weaknesses to bring us closer to him.

Sometimes, God even allows us to wait for the things we want for such a long time that we begin to believe they are impossible, just so that we might begin to understand that nothing is impossible for him.

By answering my seemingly impossible prayer for a minivan, God took my weak faith and strengthened it. He took my pathetic efforts at trust and showed me that he is not bound by the limits of human imaginations. But my story is not a new one. In the Old Testament, we read a similar story about Sarah, the wife of Abraham, who lived thousands of years ago. Sarah didn't want a minivan; she wanted a baby.

MADE FOR MOTHERHOOD

Motherhood is a core part of our feminine identity. In fact, the longing for motherhood is so deeply woven into the fabric of most women's identities that even very professionally successful women often put their career goals on hold to answer the ticking of a "biological clock" and have children. For many women, motherhood means having and raising children of their own, but for others, "motherhood" takes the form of caring for people who are not their children—siblings, parents, students, patients, neighbors, and co-workers—with the uniquely feminine gifts of nurturing love, gentleness, generosity, sensitivity, and receptivity to others. The feminine drive to nurture and care for others is built in to us. It is part of God's plan—for me, for you ... and for Sarah.

Sarah, who at the beginning of her story was known as "Sarai" (her husband was known as "Abram") knew the longing for motherhood. More than that, during the time in which she lived, bearing children was a necessity for most women's financial security. Women could hold no property of their own and therefore were dependent upon the men in their lives— husbands and sons especially—for their security. Having children raised a woman's social status, and those who were unable to conceive were pitied at best, and at worst, judged as somehow cursed by God and deserving of their unhappy state.

Perhaps you know an unfulfilled longing for motherhood in your own life. Infertility, subfertility, miscarriage, and the loss of children are forms of suffering many women have in common and have had in common since the beginning of time. One of life's deepest tragedies is that our own bodies, meant to be a gift from God and a powerful source of life-giving love, can appear to betray us sometimes. We long for a baby but can't conceive. We conceive but then lose our baby before birth. We have a child, but then, through illness, accident, or injustice, that child is taken away from us. Many women know these wounds personally, and even those of us who don't can guess at the depth of the pain they cause simply by knowing the deep-rooted desire for motherhood that is built into every one of us.

Sarai suffered the pain of infertility, a situation that not only caused her emotional pain but put her at social and financial risk as well. She knew that an heir was of great importance to her husband, and that having many descendants was considered the greatest of blessings, but with her advanced age and empty womb, that seemed an impossible dream.

A FAULTY PLAN

In her desperation, Sarai chooses not to trust in God, but instead comes up with a not-so-great plan of her own to ensure her husband will have an heir and that she will, sort of, gain the status of having a son. She arranges to give her handmaiden Hagar as a wife to Abram, so that her servant, acting as a "surrogate," might conceive and bear a son for her.

> Now Sarai, Abram's wife, bore him no children. She had an Egyptian maid whose name was Hagar; and Sarai said to Abram, "Behold now, the LORD has prevented me from bearing children; go in to my maid; it may be that I shall obtain children by her." And Abram listened to the voice of Sarai (Genesis 16:1-2).

And Sarai's plan works! Sort of.

Hagar does indeed conceive a son with Sarai's husband, but the feelings involved are a little more complicated than Sarai originally anticipated. After Hagar gives birth to Abram's son, she believes herself superior to her mistress and looks down on Sarai. Instead of gaining her status as she hoped, this newborn son now is cause for further humiliation for Sarai and proves too much to bear.

> And when [Hagar] saw that she had conceived, she looked with contempt on her mistress. And Sarai said to Abram, "May the wrong done to me be on you! I gave my maid to your embrace, and when she saw that she had conceived, she looked on me with contempt. May the LORD judge between you and me!" (Genesis 16:4-5).

Sarai clearly sees that God, who alone has the power to give her a child, is choosing not to do so, and so she takes matters into her own hands. Can we not all relate to her frustration and desperation? It may not have been about fertility for you, but every woman has felt the kind of hopelessness Sarai must feel to come up with a desperate scheme like impregnating her servant. Every one of has felt such a deep and desperate longing for something that we have considered taking drastic measures, possibly even acting outside of God's will, to get what we want.

God sees us in our hopelessness. He saw Sarai in her old age, in her impossible situation, brought upon herself by her own rash decision-making, and he loved her there, deep in her suffering, deep in her woundedness, deep in her sorrow and failing faith.

He loves you where you are, too.

GOD'S GIVES US HOPE

God reaches out to Sarai with a message of hope, delivered to her husband, Abram. It is a message of such great hope and importance that God changes Sarai and Abram's names to mark its significance. Here is what he says:

> Behold, my covenant is with you, and you shall be the father of a multitude of nations. No longer shall your name be Abram, but your name shall be Abraham; for I have made you the father of a multitude of nations. I will make you exceedingly fruitful; and I will make nations of you, and kings shall come forth from you. And I will establish my covenant between me and you and your descendants after you throughout their generations for an everlasting covenant, to be God to you and to your descendants after you (Genesis 17:4-7).

About Sarai, God says:

> As for Sarai your wife, you shall not call her name Sarai, but Sarah shall be her name. I will bless her, and moreover I will give you a son by her; I will bless her, and she shall be a mother of nations; kings of peoples shall come from her (Genesis 17:15-16).

And then, the Bible tells us, Abraham laughs. He laughs! So ridiculous does God's plan sound!

"Then Abraham fell on his face and laughed, and said to himself, 'Shall a child be born to a man who is a hundred years old? Shall Sarah, who is ninety years old, bear a child?'" (Genesis 17:17).

Abraham is not the only one who laughs. When she hears the news, so impossible does God's plan seem to Sarah, that she laughs, too.

"Sarah laughed to herself, saying, 'After I have grown old, and my husband is old, shall I have pleasure?'" (Genesis 18:12).

God does not reprimand Abraham for his laughter, but he does correct Sarah. He corrects her disbelief in order to convince her of his power and goodness. He wants her to know that he sees her in her pain, and that he is going to bless her with good things.

> The LORD said to Abraham, "Why did Sarah laugh, and say, 'Shall I indeed bear a child, now that I am old?' Is anything too hard for the LORD? At the appointed time I will return to you, in the spring, and Sarah shall have a son" (Genesis 18:13-14).

Is anything too hard for God? What desires might you have that you keep hidden away in your heart, because you wrongly believe they don't matter or are impossible even for God? Let's think of those things and give our desires to God now, as Sarah, who once felt abandoned by God in her inability to have children, learns that God has planned great blessings for her all along.

> And Sarah conceived, and bore Abraham a son in his old age at the time of which God had spoken to him ... And Sarah said, "God has made laughter for me; every one who hears will laugh over me." And she said, "Who would have said to Abraham that Sarah would suckle children? Yet I have borne him a son in his old age" (Genesis 21:2, 6-7).

The fact that Sarah's suffering takes the form of longing for a child demonstrates God's understanding and caring for the deepest desires he places in our womanly hearts. So fundamental to her identity is a woman's longing for motherhood and so, too, are all the pains she suffers due to her motherhood, that God's miraculous intervention in Sarah's fertility is all the more meaningful.

Just as God saw Sarah and the goodness of her desire to be a mother, he sees you and your desires, and he cares deeply about the things you want. The desires God places in your heart for motherhood, for love, for peace, for security, for health, and for happiness are good desires. Through Sarah's story and God's blessing of Sarah—despite her impatience and lack of faith—God affirms that he is all-knowing, all-good, and all-powerful, and that he alone can fulfill our greatest desires.

HANNAH'S HOPE

Another woman we meet in the Old Testament who longs for a child is Hannah. We meet Hannah in the first book of Samuel, where we learn that she is the wife of Elkanah, a man who loves her very much; yet Hannah is unhappy. She is unhappy because she longs for a child, and her sorrow is made all the more acute because God has seen fit to bless Elkanah's second wife, Peninnah, with many children—a fact that Peninnah, perhaps envious of her husband's love for Hannah, rubs in mercilessly.

> On the day when Elkanah sacrificed, he would give portions to Paninnah his wife and to all her sons and daughters; and, although he loved Hannah, he would give Hannah only one portion, because the LORD had closed her womb. And her

rival used to provoke her sorely, to irritate her, because the LORD had closed her womb (1 Samuel 1:4-6).

The Lord had closed her womb. These simple words emphasize God's power over our most fundamental longings and desires. God alone has the power to give the gift of motherhood or to withhold it.

In Hannah's case, he withholds it—for years. Despite her deep longing for a child, Hannah suffers the burden of infertility, and her husband's second wife torments her for it.

How many times do we allow the gifts God gives others to torment us? Even when other women do not go so far as to tease us about our lack of fertility, beauty, grace, talent, or wealth, how often do we feel belittled by the blessings God gives to others, but not to us? How often do we give way to bitterness, jealousy, and resentment in our desperate longing for the good things others enjoy?

God sees us in that struggle and takes pity on us.

God sees Hannah, too, though Hannah does not give way to bitterness against Peninnah. Hannah remains faithful and hopes in God's goodness, despite vicious teasing, but that does not mean she does not suffer. Hannah, we read, "wept and would not eat" (1 Samuel 1:7).

Even her husband's loyalty and love are not enough to make her happy.

"And Elkanah, her husband, said to her, 'Hannah, why do you weep? And why do you not eat? And why is your heart sad? Am I not more to you than ten sons?'" (1 Samuel 1:8).

These are perhaps meant to be kind words from a loving husband, but Elkanah's attempted dismissal of Hannah's pain likely makes her feel even more alone in her suffering. A loving husband is a blessing, but that does not negate the grief of longing for and not having children. Despite feeling alone and misunderstood, Hannah chooses to put her faith in God's goodness, praying more fervently than ever.

She goes to the Temple to pray. While there, she weeps and prays fervently and even makes a vow to God that if he should grant her desire for a son, she will give the child back to God by bringing him to the Temple, where he will serve God alone.

The fact that Hannah, in spite of her faithfulness, weeps as she prays demonstrates that our pain and suffering are real. Even when we trust in God and go to him in all of our wants and needs, we still sometimes suffer as we trust.

Eli, a priest at the Temple observes Hannah in prayer. She is so overcome with emotion as she prays, that he thinks she must be drunk, and he confronts her.

> But Hannah answered, "No, my lord, I am a woman sorely troubled; I have drunk neither wine nor strong drink, but I have been pouring out my soul before the LORD. Do not regard your maidservant as a base woman, for all along I have been speaking out of my great anxiety and vexation" (1 Samuel 1:15-16).

Realizing that what Hannah says is true, Eli takes pity on her and prays that God will answer her prayer.

HOPE REALIZED

God does answer Hannah's prayer, and a short time later, she becomes pregnant and gives birth to a son.

"The LORD remembered her," we read in 1 Samuel 1:19.

He remembered her. What a beautiful message of hope these words give to every woman who grieves infertility, injustice, lack of love, abuse, weakness, failure, or woundedness of any kind.

God remembered Hannah. He remembers you. He remembers me. He sees us, he knows our deepest desires, and he loves us in our longings.

God blesses Hannah's faith and hope. She hopes in the goodness of God, even when it seems impossible that she could ever have a child. And then, in her joy, Hannah continues to give us a moving example of faithfulness. God remembers Hannah, and then Hannah remembers God and the promise she made to him.

It would, of course, be terribly difficult to give up a child under any circumstances, but it would seem an almost impossibly hard thing to do for a woman who has spent years longing for the blessing of a son. Yet that is what Hannah does. Once Samuel is weaned, she brings him to the Temple where she meets with Eli, the priest.

> And she said ... "For this child I prayed; and the LORD has granted me my petition which I made to him. Therefore I have lent him to the LORD; as long as he lives, he is lent to the LORD." And they worshiped the LORD there (1 Samuel 1:26-28).

BLESSED AMONG WOMEN

Through her words and actions, Hannah demonstrates a deep faith in God's goodness and generosity. She recognizes his power over all things and knows that all good things come from him. In the chapter that follows, we read a beautiful, poetic prayer of Hannah as she praises God for his goodness and proclaims his almighty power.

> My heart exults in the LORD; my strength is exalted in the LORD. My mouth derides my enemies, because I rejoice in your salvation. There is none holy like the LORD, there is none besides you; there is no rock like our God (1 Samuel 2:1-2).

In fact, Hannah's prayer continues for many lines, and its beautiful words mirror those in a prayer that the Blessed Virgin Mary proclaims, hundreds of years later, which we read in the New Testament in the first chapter of Luke:

> My soul magnifies the Lord, and my spirit rejoices in God my Savior, for he has regarded the low estate of his handmaiden. For behold, henceforth all generations will call me blessed; for he who is mighty has done great things for me, and holy is his name (Luke 1:46-49).

Hannah's steadfast hope and faith are rivaled only by the Blessed Virgin Mary herself. God rewards Hannah's faithfulness, not only with this flattering comparison in the Bible, but with even more children. Hannah and Elkanah go on to have five more children—three sons and two daughters.

God wants to reward your hope and faith, too. But it's OK if your hope is not as impressive as Hannah's yet. Maybe you are more like Sarah, or like me with the minivan, weak and doubting, trusting in your own plans over God's sometimes and laughing at the impossibility of your desires ever truly being fulfilled.

God has plans for you just like he had for Sarah. Plans for blessing you with joy. God sees everything you want and everything you need, and he gives you hope that you will receive every good thing. God puts good desires in your heart and calls on you to trust that they will all be fulfilled by him, in the perfection of his time. Open your heart just a bit now to hear the ways in which God is calling you to be patient, to trust, and to hope in the great plans he has for you.

CLOSING PRAYER

Tender Father, you gave me more, much more
than I ever thought to ask for. I realize that
our human desires can never really match what
you long to give us. Thanks, and again thanks,
Father, for having granted my petitions, and that
which I never realized I needed or petitioned.

St. Catherine of Siena

Chapter Five

GOD BLESSES YOUR TRUST

God Knows Your Needs and Promises to Take Care of You

ANXIETY HOUR

Four o'clock in the morning is a lonely time of day. Or is it night? I am never quite sure what to call it when I find myself lying awake at that hour with my mind entertaining the worst of my anxieties. Worries never loom quite so large as they do at four in the morning when I lie wide awake, trapped between day and night.

Why does this happen? When I was younger and a rather exhausted mom, I used to brag that I could sleep anywhere. And I could! Those few quiet moments in the dentist's chair, as the hygienist scraped my teeth? I could feel a nap coming on ...

Now, it would seem that life has grown larger, and there are just so many more things to worry about, like how we will pay the dentist for that nap I took in his chair, or how we will pay for anything, really. Education, groceries, mortgages, clothing, taxes, health care—everything costs something, and bills tend to multiply and pile up at 4:00 AM, leaving me gasping for breath beneath them.

And let's not forget about the health worries. Those are a 4:00 AM favorite! Was my daughter's swollen knee really just an allergic reaction to a bug bite? Or was it perhaps the first in a series of symptoms of bone cancer? Was the headache I had earlier this week just a passing pain, or was it caused by deadly black mold that might be growing in our house? How can I be sure that my children always drive safely and never ever get in a vehicle with a friend who has been drinking? Are these heart palpitations I feel right now the beginnings of a self-induced 4:00 AM anxiety attack, or might they be the result of a carbon monoxide leak that is slowly killing my entire family?

This is serious stuff.

One of my favorite scenes in the movie *It's a Wonderful Life* is when George Bailey, desperate for a way to replace a missing $8,000, asks his guardian angel, Clarence, if he has any money. When Clarence laughs and explains that they don't use money in heaven, George's cynical response is, "Well, it comes in pretty handy down here, Bub!"

And doesn't it, though? We earthly creatures have earthly needs, and hearing about the happiness of heaven only does so much for our worries when there are bills to be paid. This is why I roll my eyes sometimes when I read one of my favorite passages from the New Testament. In the Gospel of Matthew, Jesus chides us worriers:

> And which of you by being anxious can add one cubit to his span of life? And why are you anxious about clothing? Consider the lilies of the field, how they grow; they neither toil nor spin; yet I tell you, even Solomon in all his glory was not clothed like one of these (Matthew 6:27-29).

The tenderness and encouragement we find in this passage make it one of my favorites, yet I can't help but feel like the very words are mocking me sometimes. *Because how on earth am I supposed to stop worrying?* I care a lot about a lot of stuff, OK?

And come on, Jesus, I'm actually not all that concerned about the clothing I will wear. As long as T.J. Maxx keeps putting those sweet finds on clearance, I will be fine. I don't need to be arrayed like "Solomon in all his glory." Mostly, I just want the gas bill to get paid.

SIMPLE AND SMALL

My early morning anxiety attacks betray a lack of trust. They are the result of my flawed and very human belief that God is not in charge; that I am, and I often don't feel up to the task.

In those early morning hours, as I lie awake and worry about stupid things like braces and rashes and gas bills, I often force myself to recite the words of that Bible passage over and over again, because I hear in them a call to the kind of relationship God wants us to have with him.

He wants us to trust. He wants us to be small and place ourselves in his loving care with peace in the knowledge that he will take care of all that stuff he knows we need. The birds of the air and the flowers of the field have peace. He wants us to be simple and small like they are.

EXERCISING TRUST

Years ago, when I was a young girl in third grade, I was selected to participate in an extra gym class. I don't know what earned me this honor, but two afternoons each week those of us in "gym enrichment" class met to take on physical challenges that went above and beyond the usual activities of jumping jacks and kickball that were part of our regular gym classes. We ran miles. We jumped hurdles. We practiced back flips. And one notable afternoon, we climbed "the net."

"The net" was a large web made up of thick rope that hung from the ceiling, close to the wall on one side of the gymnasium. The day we were to climb the net, we were told to each take a turn climbing to the top, stepping over the highest part of the rope, and then scaling down the other side.

The first few kids to go made it look easy, and so when my turn came, I stepped forward with confidence. After climbing just a bit, however, I made the mistake of looking down. It seemed a long way down, and my hands began to shake. I willed my legs to move further up, but they turned to jelly as I clung to the ropes in fear for my life.

"Don't look down! One step at a time!" My gym teacher called from down below. *Way* down below.

One shaky step at a time, I somehow managed to make my way further up the net. When I reached the top, though, the very idea of lifting one of my legs over to the other side was perfectly unthinkable. I froze. I gripped the ropes harder still, and the net swayed back and forth. Cold drops of sweat formed on the back of my neck.

I felt dizzy. What would happen if I fell? There was a large mat below, but I was not at all sure it would prevent a bloody and painful death. The voices of my teacher and classmates sounded very far away now, and I could not make out what they were saying.

I don't know how long I waited there, clutching the ropes at the very top of the net and refusing to move, but after what felt like a very long time, I realized that one of my classmates, Kenny, was scaling the ropes behind me.

Oh no. Kenny was the tallest and most athletic boy in our class. He had been sent to rescue me.

It was then that I realized that pride can be a more powerful motivator than self-preservation. In order to prevent what was sure to be an embarrassing rescue scene, I somehow managed to lift my leg over the top of that net. Before I knew it, I was on the other side, scrambling my way down to the sweet, sweet gym floor below.

My classmates cheered; I collapsed on the mat with relief.

I would like to visit that old gymnasium someday. I wonder if the net is still there and if kids still climb it. We did some crazy things in public school in the '70s, you know, many of which have since been prohibited for safety concerns. I wonder if the net was really as high and scary as I remember it.

I may not climb many ropes these days, but sometimes I still feel frozen, just like I did at the top of that net years ago. God sometimes calls me to things I don't feel ready for. Life can feel large and scary.

We might face challenging job situations, worries for our children, health concerns, marital crises, or the loss of loved ones. We might even lie awake and worry about these things at four in the morning. It is inside those moments, where we find ourselves called to trust in God's goodness and to step out in faith, that we can feel ourselves frozen with fear.

Do you ever struggle to trust? Do you ever feel scared and alone, left at the top of a net, not knowing how to get over to the other side?

It is in those moments that God calls on each of us to trust him. He knows it's hard for us to do, but he calls us to trust him anyway. He wants us to know the kind of peace and joy that can only be found in trusting him completely, and with everything.

The good news is that we don't have to trust alone. Others have gone before us, going back thousands of years. Many women have stepped out in faith and trusted in God's goodness, and we can read their stories in the Old Testament. As we read, we can learn the ways God rewards our trust, especially in our most vulnerable moments. Two women that especially inspire us with their examples of trust in God, even in dire situations, are the widow of Zarephath and the Shunammite woman.

ALMOST EMPTY

We meet the widow of Zarephath in 1 Kings, when the prophet Elijah pays her a visit. We don't know her name, but we know that God himself chose her to play an important role in the story of Elijah.

"Then the word of the LORD came to him, 'Arise, go to Zarephath, which belongs to Sidon, and dwell there. Behold, I have commanded a widow there to feed you'" (1 Kings 17:8-9).

Where Elijah was going and the people he would interact with were important details because he was a prophet on the run. King Ahab and Queen Jezebel were angry with him for an incident where he killed many false prophets of their pagan religion, and they were chasing him in order to kill him.

God knew that no one would suspect that a great and mighty prophet would be found dwelling in the house of a poor and lowly widow, and so the widow of Zarephath was chosen for this great task.

When Elijah finds the widow, she is gathering sticks for a fire, and he asks her to bring him some water. As she leaves to fetch the water, he adds one more request:

"Bring me a morsel of bread in your hand" (1 Kings 17:11).

The widow does not refuse Elijah's request, but she does explain the difficult situation it puts her in.

And she said, "As the LORD your God lives, I have nothing baked, only a handful of meal in a jar, and a little oil in a cruse; and now, I am gathering a couple of sticks, that I may go and prepare it for myself and my son, that we may eat it, and die" (1 Kings 17:12).

I am always struck by the calm manner with which this woman explains that she is preparing one last meal before starving to death with her son. She is destitute. When Elijah asks her to give him some of what little she has left, she could respond with anger or hysteria. Instead, though, she calmly explains that it will be difficult to do what he asks.

Have you ever felt that God was asking too much from you? Have you ever felt like you have nothing left to give—just a handful of meal and a few drops of oil—and God asks for more? Through your family, work, or life circumstances, does it ever feel like God is asking for more than you have to give? It doesn't feel fair sometimes, does it?

I'm sure the widow of Zarephath feels Elijah's request for a share of her meager food supplies is not exactly fair, but she complies with his request.

His words of reassurance to her in this moment, where he calls her to generosity, are similar to ones we hear from Jesus, later in the New Testament:

"Fear not," Elijah says to her.

"Fear not," Jesus says to us, over and over again.[1]

Yet it is so hard not to be afraid.

---

[1]   See Matthew 6:34, 10:28; Mark 4:39-40, 5:36, 6:50; Luke 12:22-26; John 14:27.

Elijah tells the widow to prepare him a little cake and then to prepare food for herself and her son.

> For thus says the Lord the God of Israel, "The jar of meal shall not be spent, and the cruse of oil shall not fail, until the day that the Lord sends rain upon the earth. And she went and did as Elijah said; and she, and he, and her household ate for many days. The jar of meal was not spent, neither did the cruse of oil fail, according to the word of the Lord which he spoke by Elijah" (1 Kings 17:14-16).

The widow is rewarded because she trusts in God's goodness and obeys him, even when she is afraid. She trusts in God to provide for what she and her son need, and indeed he does. Miraculously, for many days, she, Elijah, and her son eat from a tiny supply of meal and oil that never seems to run out.

Is your jar of oil running low? Do you live in fear of losing what little you have?

Especially during times in our lives when we feel like we are "running on empty," God calls on us to trust in him. Trusting God is not a guarantee that nothing bad will happen, but it does enable us to grow in the kind of dependent relationship God wants us to have with him. He wants us to stop trusting in our bank accounts, jobs, spouses, and even our own work to provide for us, and instead turn to him in our every need. He always rewards that kind of trust.

ASKING STILL MORE

The widow of Zarephath not only trusts God when her food supplies ran low, but she has yet another opportunity to trust God, through Elijah, when something even more dramatic happens.

> After this the son of the woman, the mistress of the house, became ill; and his illness was so severe that there was no breath left in him. And she said to Elijah, "What have you against me, O man of God? You have come to me to bring my sin to remembrance, and to cause the death of my son!" And he said to her, "Give me your son." And he took him from her bosom, and carried him up into the upper chamber, where he lodged, and laid him upon his own bed (1 Kings 17:17-19).

Elijah calls upon God to save the boy, and his prayer is answered.

"And the LORD hearkened to the voice of Elijah; and the soul of the child came into him again, and he revived" (1 Kings 17:22).

Notice that in this story, we read that Elijah takes the widow's son "from her bosom." Can't you just imagine her, holding her dead child, the most precious thing to her on this earth, and clutching him to her chest? He is precious to her, yet she lets go of him. She hands her precious child over to Elijah, trusting him to heal her son through the power of God.

What might you be "clutching to your chest," hesitant to give over to God, trusting in his goodness?

We sometimes cling to things like wealth, status, achievement, material goods, earthly pleasures, or human relationships to fulfill our needs. We cling to them and place our trust in these fleeting things instead of in God himself. What might God be asking you to let go of and hand over to him?

It was hard for the widow to share her last bits of food. It was hard for her to hand over her precious child. It is hard for us, too. God knows that, and so he calls us gently and waits patiently, reminding us all the while not to fear.

THE SHUNAMMITE WOMAN

Later in the Old testament, we meet another unnamed woman who opens her home to a prophet. This time it is a Shunammite woman who welcomes the prophet Elisha and gives him a place to stay.

Unlike the widow of Zarephath, the Shunammite woman is wealthy and seemingly powerful. She believes Elisha is a man of God, and she wants to make sure he is always welcome and has a place to stay in her home.

> And she said to her husband, "Behold now, I perceive that this is a holy man of God, who is continually passing our way. Let us make a small roof chamber with walls, and put there for him a bed, a table, a chair, and a lamp, so that whenever he comes to us, he can go in there" (2 Kings 4:9-10).

Elisha so appreciates this kindness and hospitality that he wants to repay the Shunamite woman in some way. He sends his servant, Gehazi, to find out what the woman might need. Gehazi suggests that maybe he can help the woman attain some kind of status with powerful people in her community.

> When he had called her, she stood before him. And he said … "See, you have taken all this trouble for us; what is to be done for you? Would you have a word spoken on your behalf to the king or to the commander of the army?" She answered. "I dwell among my own people" (2 Kings 4:12-13).

I love how straightforward her answer is: "I dwell among my own people."

In other words, she is quite comfortable and does not need any kind of help or status Elisha might offer. These are words of contentment, yet there really is something the Shunammite woman wants. She wants it so desperately that she does not dare even to entertain the thought of her desire being fulfilled.

The Shunammite woman wants a child. Though she enjoys wealth, power, and status, she and her aging husband have no children. She wants a child so desperately, in fact, that she does not speak of her longing. She has put the possibility of motherhood out of her mind to protect herself from the potential pain of disappointment. It is too painful to even consider the possibility of motherhood.

We see a hint of her pain and her longing, however, when Elisha calls to her to tell her she will be blessed with a son.

> He said, "Call her." And when he had called her, she stood in the doorway. And he said, "At this season, when the time comes round, you shall embrace a son." And she said, "No, my lord, O man of God; do not lie to your maidservant" (2 Kings 4:15-16).

NOT SO SELF-SUFFICIENT

The Shunammite woman wants a child so very badly that she almost cannot bear to hear the words spoken to her. To protect her feelings and shield herself from the pain of disappointment, she does not allow herself even to hope for a child.

And yet God sees her deep, unspoken longing, and through the prayers of Elisha, he fulfills her greatest desires by blessing her with a son.

When Elisha asks what the woman needs, she replies that she does not need anything. In many ways this is true, as she enjoys many good things. It can be good to cultivate contentedness with the good things we have. But when we have many good things, it can be tempting to think we don't need God for much of anything.

The story of the Shunammite woman opens our eyes to the fact that we sometimes might hide behind our self-sufficiency. Out of fear and insecurity, we sometimes fail to trust God with our greatest desires, wrongly thinking he cannot possibly fulfill them.

What are you holding back? In what ways are you afraid of being hurt or disappointed? What deep longings are you afraid to give voice to? What desires are you reluctant to share, even with God?

TESTING HER TRUST

Perhaps our trust in God can be strengthened by reading on in the story about the Shunammite woman and learning the next way in which her trust is tested, this time with her son.

> When the child had grown, he went out one day to his father among the reapers. And he said to his father, "Oh, my head, my head!" The father said to his servant, "Carry him to his mother." And when he had lifted him, and brought him to his mother, the child sat in her lap till noon, and then he died (2 Kings 4:18-20).

Wait, what? Why on earth did we go through all of that? Did God really bless this faithful woman by fulfilling her deep, unspoken desire for a child, only to take away that child later on, through a mysterious and tragic death?

The Shunammite woman appears to be asking many of these same questions herself. Devastated, she lays her dead son in Elisha's room and saddles up her donkey to go to him as quickly as she can.

> And when she came to the mountain to the man of God, she caught hold of his feet. And Gehazi came to thrust her away. But the man of God said, "Let her alone, for she is in bitter distress; and the LORD has hidden it from me, and has not told me." Then she said, "Did I ask my lord for a son? Did I not say, Do not deceive me?" (2 Kings 4:27-28).

What she has feared has come to pass. By accepting the gift of her son, the Shunammite woman has made herself vulnerable to the pain of loss. In her bitter sorrow, she reminds Elisha that she did not ask for a son, that she never would have spoken this desire, and that she could have lived on in contentment with her many blessings.

In other words, she did not ask for this.

Do you ever feel this way? Do you ever feel that life has thrown you for a loop by setting you on a path you never would have chosen for yourself? Do you sometimes find yourself suffering as a result of life circumstances that are beyond your control, and even suffering because of the loss of good things you never even asked for?

The Shunammite woman feels this pain acutely, and yet she trusts God. Somehow, perhaps through the blessing of her son, she seems to have grown in her trust in the goodness of God through Elisha, a man she believes does the work of God.

Note that when the woman goes to Elisha, she takes hold of his feet. Consider the idea of throwing yourself down and holding onto another person's feet. This is a gesture of great humility, dependence, and trust. Through Elisha, the Shunammite woman places herself completely at the mercy of God.

And God rewards her trust. Elisha goes to her house and prays over her dead son, and he comes back to life.

> Then he summoned Gehazi and said, "Call this Shunammite." So he called her. And when she came to him, he said, "Take up your son." She came and fell at his feet, bowing to the ground; then she took up her son and went out (2 Kings 4:36-37).

These two dramatic stories of life and death reveal something true about the human experience. We may not always recognize it, but we are all always completely dependent upon the mercy of God. Especially when things go well for us, it can be tempting to think we need only rely on ourselves and that we can attain all we desire through our own hard work and virtue.

But the truth is that we are all helpless. Every one of us is only a breath away from tragedy and devastation at any moment. We all must rely completely on God for every good thing we have, from hearts beating in our chests, to air filling our lungs, to the most basic of necessities like food, clothing, and shelter. All of it comes to us only through the goodness and mercy of God.

It can be frightening to throw ourselves at God's feet and trust in him, but when we do, God rewards our faithfulness. God tells us the stories of the widow of Zarephath and the Shunammite woman in the Bible so that we might read them and know that we are made for him. Through these stories, we can come to know that we are called to that kind of trust in the goodness of God, even when it's hard (especially when it's hard).

It's OK if you find yourself lying awake at four in the morning. It's OK if you feel caught in an impossible situation sometimes, alone and scared, at the top of a high net with nowhere to go. In moments like these, let us remember the women who have gone before us. May we find in their stories the strength to throw ourselves at God's feet and trust in his goodness.

You can make the choice to trust God now. Trust him to give you every good thing, even those things you are afraid to ask for. In his goodness, mercy, and love, God, who knows everything you need, will see you and bless your trust in him.

CLOSING PRAYER

Let nothing disturb you. Let nothing frighten you.
All things are passing away: God never changes.
Patience obtains all things. Whoever has God
lacks nothing; God alone suffices.

– St. Teresa of Avila

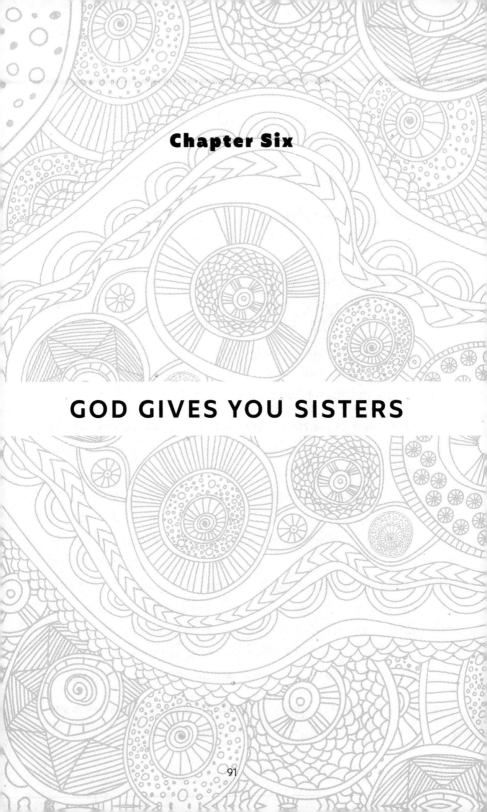

Chapter Six

GOD GIVES YOU SISTERS

God Gives You the Gift of Friendship and Connection with Others

BLOOD SISTERS

Krissy lived next door to the house I grew up in. She was one year older, and throughout much of our childhood, the two of us were inseparable. We rode bikes together, went swimming at the local pool, built snowmen, and went sledding in the winter. I remember one day in particular, when I was about eight years old. I accidentally cut my hand with a pair of scissors and then spent the next two hours wandering the neighborhood looking for Krissy, because this was our big chance to become "blood sisters."

Krissy is a nurse today and likely would disapprove of the concept of "blood sisters," but nonetheless, I am sure she recognizes the gift that our close friendship was to each of us, especially as we grew older and our perspectives and experiences began to change in significant ways. As preteens and teens, the two of us would sit in our backyard treehouse after school, doing our nails and discussing important things, like how embarrassing it was to be getting our period on the day of Jessica's big pool party and which boys we liked and which boys we thought might like us. These were intensely personal topics that I never discussed with anyone else, but somehow, with Krissy, it was safe to talk about anything.

We all need a friendship like that, because there are some things only a girlfriend, a sister, can understand.

SOUL SISTERS

Besides my "sisterhood" with Krissy, I was blessed to grow up with three biological sisters as well. With each of them, I have happy memories of playing dolls, roller skating, and hosting tea parties, as well as some embarrassing memories of fighting over the hairdryer. We were normal sisters, after all.

I shared a room with my sister Hélène, who was two years older than me, and in many ways throughout my childhood, I idolized her. It was like watching a movie reel of a future life I hoped for. I watched with awe as she struggled through algebra, knowing that in two years' time it would be my turn to attempt mixing the alphabet with numbers. I watched her star in school plays and wondered at her talent and confidence. And I watched her graduate high school and leave for college all the way across the country. The day she left for the airport, I said goodbye to her in the driveway and then ran inside to lock myself in our room and cry.

Years later, Hélène got married and became a mother, and like always, I followed in her footsteps, just a couple years of years behind. In every struggle of new motherhood, I found myself turning to my older sister over and over again for the wisdom of her experience and the understanding only our shared upbringing could provide. We have shared motherhood moments similarly with our two younger sisters over the years as well.

KNOWN AND LOVED

One Easter Sunday just a few years ago, the four of us grown-up sisters were in my parents' kitchen, fussing over plates of ham and potatoes as the chaos of a large family gathering swirled around us, filling my parents' home with noisy commotion. In the midst of our conversations, time and again, we sisters found ourselves saying the exact same things, at the exact same times, with eerily similar voices and intonations. It was like being in a room with three slightly varied versions of myself.

Once, when my sister Christine left a voicemail on my mother's phone, wishing her a happy birthday, my mom called each of us to say thank you, because she could not tell which of her daughters had left the message.

In this kind of closeness and identification with other women, there is the blessing of being known, understood, loved, and accepted.

We all long to be known and understood like that, and no one can know us and understand us quite like our sisters can. Biological sisters, adopted sisters, "blood" sisters, and sisters in Christ. The kind of bonds that women create in authentic friendships with one another simply cannot be replicated in other kinds of relationships. You might be married, and you might rightly call your husband your best friend, but there are some things only a girlfriend can understand.

Because we "get" each other in ways most men cannot fully understand, women are uniquely capable of encouraging, affirming, and supporting one another. We have gifts of sensitivity, compassion, and intuition that make us capable of truly understanding one another in ways that sometimes leave others standing in bewilderment on the sidelines.

Our sisterhood with other women is a powerful thing. It is because we are capable of knowing each other so intimately that no one can tear a woman apart quite like another woman can. Many of us have seen or suffered the damage caused by toxic female friendships, vicious gossip, competition, or jealousy.

While it is true that women can be proficient at tearing one another apart, the happy truth is that the opposite is equally true: There is no one who can build up, affirm, and encourage a woman quite like another woman can. Women are such a gift to one another!

One of my favorite scenes in the Bible is the one where Mary, Jesus' Mother, shows us the power and importance of female friendships. When Mary learns that her cousin Elizabeth is pregnant, we read in Luke:

"Mary arose and went with haste into the hill country, to a city of Judah, and she entered the house of Zechariah and greeted Elizabeth" (Luke 1:39-40).

She went *with haste.* There are no accidental or extra words in the Bible, and I love that these particular words are included here. This was important; Mary wasn't messing around.

The fact that Mary went "with haste" to attend to her cousin in her time of need speaks to the importance of the action she took. Girlfriends are important. The kind of mutual support, encouragement, and understanding uniquely found inside of female friendships is important.

Even if Mary had pressing concerns of her own (having just learned she was to be the mother of the Messiah), she still went "with haste" to support and celebrate her cousin's special life event as well. We can truly imagine the depth of beauty and meaning in the scene that followed. Elizabeth's words of joy upon seeing Mary are so authentic and filled with joy that we Catholics still remember them and pray them today, thousands of years later:

"Blessed are you among women, and blessed is the fruit of your womb!" (Luke 1:42).

We don't have to wait for Jesus' arrival to find powerful examples of female cooperation, connection, and friendship in the Bible. Many of our sisters went before us, setting an example of feminine friendship and sisterhood, getting it right and getting it wrong, in ways that still speak to us about the gift of girlfriends today, thousands of years later.

In the Old Testament, we find stories of female friendships and sisters who work together bravely to overcome institutionalized injustice, who fight bitterly when pitted against one another, and who inspire us with their generosity, loyalty, and love for one another, even through the toughest of times.

One of the most memorable stories of female friendship we encounter early in the Old Testament is when a young girl and a princess conspire to take a stand against injustice and save an innocent baby's life.

MIRIAM AND THE PRINCESS

Everyone knows the stories about Moses in the Bible. In grade school religious education classes, we learn about the guy who went up the mountain and returned with the Ten Commandments etched on stone tablets. Heck, there have been entire movies made about Moses!

Did you know that none of that could have happened were it not for the brave actions of a young girl and a woman, strangers to one another, who conspired against an unjust law together?

The time when Moses was born was a dangerous time to be a Hebrew male infant. The Egyptian king, fearing the vigor and strength of God's people, commanded that every male Hebrew baby should be killed. Moses' mother managed to hide him for the first three months of his life, but as he grew older, she feared being discovered.

> And when she could hide him no longer she took for him a basket made of bulrushes, and daubed it with bitumen and pitch; and she put the child in it and placed it among the reeds at the river's brink. And his sister stood at a distance, to know what would be done to him (Exodus 2:3-4).

The older sister was Miriam, and it is estimated she was about six years old at the time that her brother Moses was left in a basket in the river. Miriam was a young girl, but old enough to grasp the dangers of the world and to be concerned for her baby brother's welfare.

Perhaps her mother gave her the job of watching over baby Moses, or perhaps this was a responsibility she felt called to take on by herself. Either way, what happens next is a moving example of feminine strength and cooperation standing up against terrible injustice to protect the innocent. And it reads like a fairy-tale, with a princess and all!

The Pharaoh's daughter, a princess, comes to the river to bathe. She notices Moses' basket floating in the reeds nearby and sends her maid to fetch it. She hears the baby cry, opens the basket, and discovers baby Moses inside. Immediately, she knows that this baby must be a Hebrew child, abandoned by his mother, in the hope that she might save his life.

WORKING TOGETHER AGAINST EVIL

Think of how young Miriam's heart must have been racing upon seeing a princess discover her brother, perhaps fearing that he would be killed and not knowing how to save him.

What she does next takes cleverness and courage. She comes out of hiding, approaches the princess, and offers to find a nursemaid for the baby. Of course, the princess will need someone to feed the infant! And of course, Miriam is thinking of her mother, Moses' own mother, for this task. In this way, the family might be reunited under the protection of the princess' desire to keep the baby. The princess agrees, and Miriam fetches her mother for the job.

The courage of women, especially when working together in the face of injustice, is a theme of this chapter in the Bible. First, we read about the midwives who "fear God" and conspire together to defy the Pharaoh's order to kill all male Hebrew children, explaining that Hebrew women are strong and give birth too quickly for them to arrive on the scene. No one questions this explanation, and many babies are spared a cruel death because of it.

Then we read about Miriam, small and brave, who hides in the bushes, not knowing what she can do to protect her brother but feeling called to stay near him to find out. When the princess discovers the baby, she, like the midwives before her, is also moved to "work around" Pharaoh's evil order, and Miriam's courageous suggestion offers her the perfect opportunity.

In this way, Miriam and the princess become "sisters" of sorts in their conspiracy to save baby Moses. They come together, each motivated to overcome injustice. God uses their cooperation to save Moses, and as a consequence, to save all of the Hebrew people from the slavery Moses would free them from years later.

When women work together, evil cannot prevail. There is simply no match for our cooperative feminine strength, cunning, and courage.

SATAN'S DISTRACTIONS

It is a testament to the power and strength of our sisterly bonds that Satan himself can't seem to resist meddling in our relationships sometimes. It is telling that this, one of the strongest of human bonds, woman to woman, has the potential to become one of the bitterest of rivalries—derailed by envy, suspicion, jealousy, and competition.

We find a prime example of sisterly bonds gone awry in the relationship between Rachel and Leah, real-life sisters who fight over and share everything ... including a husband.

In Genesis 29, we meet Jacob, who in his travels, comes across the land, flocks, and family of Laban, whom he soon discovers is his mother's brother. Rachel and Leah, Laban's daughters, are his cousins. Upon this discovery, there is a family reunion of sorts with much joy.

> Then Jacob kissed Rachel, and wept aloud. And Jacob told Rachel that he was her father's kinsman ... and she ran and told her father. When Laban heard the tidings of Jacob his sister's son, he ran to meet him, and embraced him and kissed him, and brought him to his house ... Laban said to him, "Surely, you are my bone and my flesh!" And he stayed with him a month (Genesis 29:11-14).

During his stay with Laban and his family, Jacob falls in love with Rachel. Leah is the older of the two sisters, but she has some kind of physical ailment that affects her eyes, while Rachel is healthy, younger, and more attractive.

"Leah's eyes were weak, but Rachel was beautiful and lovely" (Genesis 29:17).

RIVALRY AND DECEPTION

Given the sisters' closeness, you can probably imagine that some level of rivalry already exists between the two. Imagine growing up being known as the sister with "weak eyes," while your younger sister, "beautiful and lovely," gets all the attention. Whatever rivalry or resentment already exists is only made worse by their father's actions in the next part of the story.

Laban intends to keep Jacob in his household as a worker, and when he asks him what he wants for his wages, Jacob asks to be given the younger, more beautiful daughter (Rachel) as his wife. The two men agree that Jacob will work for Laban for seven years in exchange for receiving Rachel in marriage.

Jacob is so in love with Rachel that the years go by quickly.

"So Jacob served seven years for Rachel, and they seemed to him but a few days because of the love he had for her" (Genesis 29:20).

Imagine the older, weaker, less attractive sister, Leah, as she watches Jacob's steadfast love and devotion to her younger sister, while no man comes for her. There must be feelings of resentment brewing already by the time seven years passes and the wedding day arrives.

And what a wedding it is! With a surprise bride and everything ...

> So Laban gathered together all the men of the place, and made a feast. But in the evening he took his daughter Leah and brought her to Jacob; and he went in to her ... And in the morning, behold, it was Leah; and Jacob said to Laban. "What is this you have done to me? Did I not serve with you for Rachel? Why then have you deceived me?" Laban said, "It is not so done in our country, to give the younger before the first-born" (Genesis 29:22-26).

Oh, is that all, Laban? It's not customary to marry off the younger daughter first, so instead of talking to Jacob about this socially awkward situation, you switch out the bride and trick him into marrying your other daughter? This is amazing stuff.

Jacob, shockingly, seems to take all of this in stride and agrees to keep Leah as his wife and work another seven years to earn Rachel as his second wife.

I remember reading these shenanigans in my Bible story book as a young child with my jaw hanging open. The dad switched out his daughters and faked the bride? The older daughter went along with it? What on earth was happening here?

What, indeed. Of course, during this time period, women for the most part did whatever the men in their lives told them to do, but the fact that we read of no protest from Leah in being part of the plot to steal her sister's husband is telling. She was perhaps acting upon jealous feelings that had been festering for the last seven years while she watched Jacob's devotion and love for her sister Rachel—the beautiful one.

The Bible tells us nothing of Rachel's feelings when she learns of this wedding day charade. She has likely spent the last seven years enjoying Jacob's attention and looking forward to the day they would be married. To find out now that because of her father's scheming, her sister has become Jacob's wife instead, and that it will be another seven years before she can marry him (and that she will forever be his "second wife")? This story rivals even the wildest of soap opera plots.

RESENTMENT GROWS DEEPER

Nonetheless, Jacob completes his years of service and earns the right to marry Rachel in addition to Leah. Then the sisterly rivalry really begins as Leah conceives and bears sons with Jacob, but Rachel suffers infertility.

There is sadness and longing for love, though, even inside of Leah's joy in bearing children.

> When the LORD saw that Leah was hated, he opened her womb; but Rachel was barren. And Leah conceived and bore a son, and she called his name Reuben; for she said, "Because the LORD has looked upon my affliction; surely now my husband will love me" (Genesis 29:31-32).

With each subsequent son she gives birth to, we read of Leah's longing for love. Each time, she speaks of her hope of finally receiving Jacob's love, but each time she is disappointed. Jacob, after all, loves only Rachel.

But Rachel, for her part, appears equally miserable.

> When Rachel saw that she bore Jacob no children, she
> envied her sister; and she said to Jacob, "Give me children,
> or I shall die!" Jacob's anger was kindled against Rachel, and
> he said, "Am I in the place of God, who has withheld from
> you the fruit of the womb?" (Genesis 30:1-2).

One sister has children and longs for her husband's love. The
other sister has her husband's love and longs for children.
Each sister suffers feelings of resentment and envy as a result
of her own unhappiness.

The series of events that follows becomes a sort of "baby-
producing" competition between the two sisters. It is very
weird (at least from a modern perspective), and it gets ugly.

Growing desperate to in some way provide Jacob with sons
herself, Rachel encourages him to sleep with her maid.
When her maid conceives and bears a son not just once but
twice, providing two sons for Jacob, Rachel feels that she has
triumphed over Leah.

"Then Rachel said, 'With mighty wrestlings I have wrestled
with my sister, and have prevailed'; so she called his name
Naphtali" (Genesis 30:8).

Seeing her sister's triumph and having ceased bearing any
children herself (perhaps because Jacob, who does not love
her, has stopped sleeping with her), Leah decides it is time
she offered her maid to Jacob as well. As a result, Leah's
maid bears a son.

Each time a new baby is born, the two sisters name their
children and the children of their maids with names that
announce how blessed and happy they are. They use names
that mean "Good fortune!" and "Happy am I!"

But these joyful names can only contrast with the real sense of sadness, longing, and lack of love that both women experience as a result of their rivalry.

In a further bizarre twist in the story, we read of some wheeling and dealing between the two sisters. Rachel wants mandrakes that Leah's son Reuben has, presumably to cure her of her infertility, and so she strikes a deal with her sister: She will allow her to sleep with Jacob again in exchange for the mandrakes. It appears that the women, at least in matters of sexual intimacy, have complete control over their situations. Jacob returns to Leah, and, as a result, Leah gives birth to two more sons and a daughter. Is your head spinning yet?

GOD REMEMBERS

At this point, after all this baby-producing by means of other women, fortune finally changes for Rachel.

"Then God remembered Rachel, and God hearkened to her and opened her womb" (Genesis 30:22).

I like to reflect on the poignancy of these words—*God remembered Rachel.* Even in the midst of the ugly competition between Rachel and her sister, God remembers her. There, in the midst of her misery, God takes pity on her and blesses her with what she longs for the most.

He takes pity on us, too. When we grow distracted by rivalries and jealousy with our sisters, whether biological sisters or simply the women God has placed in our lives—women who are meant to be a gift and a blessing to us—God is there in the mess with us. Even if we are petty and small sometimes, he does not abandon us.

Imagine the unique joy Leah and Rachel might have shared together as sisters, if they had chosen to love and support one another in their trying circumstances, despite the temptation toward envy. Instead, they chose the easy path of succumbing to competition and resentment, and it did not turn out to be so easy after all. Because of their selfishness in relation to one another, they both suffered a loss of the support they might have found in one another, but they also missed out on the joy God meant for them to find in their marriages and motherhood. Even as they named their babies happy and blessed names, neither of them ever really enjoys their family life.

Women are meant to be a gift to one another. The women present in our lives, whether we have chosen them as our girlfriends or we were born with them as our sisters, are meant to be a source of encouragement, affirmation, and support for us. There will always be the temptation to compare ourselves to other women and to compete with them for male attention, or "success" in work or motherhood, but we are called to be better than that.

Two women who answered the call to sisterhood by setting a shining example of loyalty and love for the rest of us come along a bit later in the Old Testament. We meet Ruth and her mother-in-law, Naomi, years later, in the book of Ruth.

IN-LAWS, LOYALTY, AND LOVE

In-law relationships can be tricky. When two women are connected not by blood, but by marriage only, there is significant room for conflict. I remember feeling keenly the tension between my husband's mother and me even before my husband and I were married. Thankfully, we navigated it without any major issues, but I knew the potential for conflict was there. Perhaps you have felt a similar tension between yourself and a mother-in-law, sister-in-law, or daughter-in-law in your family.

As we witnessed in the story of Leah and Rachel, there is an inevitable sense of rivalry when two females attempt to share the affection of one male. The fact that the one male is son to one of the women and husband to the other matters little. Two women plus one man just equals trouble.

But when taken on in the right spirit, in-law relationships can be a wonderful source of enrichment, support, love, and blessings multiplied. I have a friend Kim who claims she "won the lottery" when it comes to mothers-in-law. Over the course of her twenty-three-year marriage, Kim's mother-in-law has been a go-to resource for her entire family. She is always ready to help with laundry, babysitting, or dishes, and she offers a sympathetic ear or gentle words of advice, borne of her own years of experience, whenever needed. Because of the generous spirit of their relationship, Kim is eager to support and care for her mother-in-law in whatever ways are needed in the years to come, when age might cause health issues and other challenges.

The beauty of female bonds like my friend Kim's with her mother-in-law is that they demonstrate for us the power that female friendships have to lift us up and accomplish good things in the lives of our families. When women generously encourage, support, and help each other, everyone benefits.

Our long-ago sisters Naomi and Ruth first become connected through marriage. Because of a famine, Naomi and her husband, along with their two sons, move to Moab. There, the two sons are married, and so two new women, Orpah and Ruth, join the family.

Soon after, presumably because of the famine, all three men die, leaving the three women, none of them related by blood, alone and in a desperate situation. Because women could not own property at the time, Naomi, a woman who has lost her husband and her two sons, finds herself in a particularly challenging situation, with no means of providing for herself.

She decides to return to Bethlehem, in order to escape the famine and seek food. But Naomi knows that she is a liability to her daughters-in-law. She understands that they are young enough to marry again and could find a measure of security for themselves that she cannot. Thus, she urges them to leave her.

> But Naomi said to her two daughters-in-law, "Go, return each of you to her mother's house. May the LORD deal kindly with you, as you have dealt with the dead and with me. The LORD grant that you may find a home, each of you in the house of her husband!" Then she kissed them, and they lifted up their voices and wept (Ruth 1:8-9).

These are women that have suffered terrible loss together and now face an uncertain future, perhaps in separation. Perhaps you have experienced the closeness that can come from sharing your wounds with another woman. There is bonding in weeping together. We can feel the love they have for one another in the description of their sorrow.

After much persuasion, Orpah does decide to leave Naomi and return to her family. No one can blame her for this. It is actually a very reasonable thing for her to do in light of her difficult circumstances.

Ruth, however, refuses to leave Naomi and remains loyal to her mother-in-law in her time of need. She professes her devotion to Naomi in a dramatic way.

> Entreat me not to leave you or to return from following you; for where you go I will go, and where you lodge I will lodge; your people shall be my people, and your God my God; where you die I will die, and there will I be buried. May the LORD do so to me and more also if even death parts me from you (Ruth 1:16-17).

A NEW BEGINNING

Note that in her poetic speech, Ruth declares loyalty not only to Naomi, but to her people and her God as well. She has undergone a real conversion of heart and thus her journey to Bethlehem marks a new beginning in her life. And we will see the ways in which God blesses her decision to trust and love generously.

Naomi and Ruth arrive in Bethlehem at the beginning of the barley harvest. Ruth, ready and willing to do whatever she can to provide for herself and for Naomi, asks for permission to glean in the fields after the reapers have taken what they can. This is a very humble proposal, to follow in the footsteps of harvesters and collect whatever scraps of food might be left. But Ruth knows that those small bits of food can add up to lifesaving meals for her and Naomi in their desperate situation, and so she works diligently to collect them.

Boaz, a wealthy man who owns the fields, notices Ruth's hard work and asks about her. He finds out the whole story of her loyalty to Naomi, who happens to be a distant relative of his, and he decides to reward Ruth for her loyalty and hard work.

He calls for her and gives her special permission to collect even more food from the fields in choice locations and invites her to eat and drink with his servants.

Overcome with gratitude, Ruth falls on her face and bows before Boaz, asking why he treats her with such kindness.

> But Boaz answered her, "All that you have done for your mother-in-law since the death of your husband has been fully told me, and how you left your father and mother and your native land and came to a people that you did not know before. The LORD recompense you for what you have done, and a full reward be given you by the LORD, the God of Israel, under whose wings you have come to take refuge!" (Ruth 2:11-12).

Overjoyed, Ruth returns to Naomi to tell her all that has happened. Naomi, recognizing that Boaz is a kind man of means, sees an even greater opportunity for Ruth.

Like a good mother-in-law should, Naomi starts scheming, and she "works the system" just a bit, in order to secure a beneficial marriage for Ruth. She instructs Ruth to dress in her best clothes and go lie at Boaz's feet while he sleeps. Ruth, not fully understanding the significance of what her mother-in-law suggests, trusts Naomi and obeys.

When Boaz is surprised to find Ruth lying at his feet, he understands immediately that this is a suggestion of marriage, and he is flattered by the request, as Naomi likely knew he would be.

"And he said, 'May you be blessed by the Lord, my daughter; you have made this last kindness greater than the first, in that you have not gone after young men, whether poor or rich'" (Ruth 3:10).

As a relative of Ruth's deceased husband, Boaz has a right to take Ruth as his wife, and eventually this is what he does. Ruth bears a son, who thus is considered a descendent of Naomi who previously had no hope for more children. The two women's financial woes are over as all has gone according to the plan of Naomi, the scheming mother-in-law who has found a way to return Ruth's kindness.

IMPORTANCE OF RELATIONSHIP

The story of the friendship between Naomi and Ruth is especially meaningful to us as women because it emphasizes the importance of female relationships. There is no flashy plot line in their story—no wars won or battles fought. Theirs is simply a story of steadfast love and loyalty between two women. It's a story made up of small gestures of kindness, moments of generosity, and unlikely heroines taking on daunting challenges, united in sisterly love.

We women know the importance of small stuff like this because, more so than men, we are wired for human connection. We are built for communion and relationship with others. The touching story of Ruth and Naomi's love for one another is testament to the unique strength we women have when we connect with and care for one another.

Ruth uses her God-given feminine strength of generosity and hard work in service to Naomi, Naomi uses her God-given feminine strength of cunning and understanding of human interactions to help set up Ruth for a beneficial marriage. Together, the two women share a unique bond of love and friendship that inspires even people observing from the outside, and even people reading about it thousands of years later.

Do you have friendships like Ruth and Naomi's? Do you know that God means for you to find support from the women he places in your life, and that he means for you to be a means of support to other women as well?

You may not have biological sisters to share your life with, but every one of us has women in our lives that are put there for a purpose.

You have a unique calling to love and encourage other women in your life as well as to find love and encouragement for yourself inside of those relationships. You alone have the power to choose how you will approach relationships with women in your life and the effect you will allow them to have on you and your family.

Will you find in your sisters here on earth the unique source of encouragement, affirmation, and support God means for your female friendships to be? Or will you allow yourself to be derailed by comparison, jealousy, and competition?

Sisterhood is a gift from God. Every woman is a gift for other women. How will you be that gift and receive that gift in your life today?

CLOSING PRAYER

Loving one another with the charity of Christ,
let the love you have in your hearts be shown
outwardly in your deeds so that compelled by such
an example, the sisters may also grow in the love
of God and charity for one another.

St. Clare of Assisi

Chapter Seven

GOD MADE YOU FOR LIFE-GIVING LOVE

God Blesses Others with the Gift of You

HARD-WORKING HANDS

My mother's hands flew as she worked beside me. She rolled dough, filled plates, and crimped crusts. She lined the counter with uniform pie shells with crisp edges, filled them with lemon custard, and then began whipping egg whites into meringue.

I sprinkled the kitchen table with spoonfuls of flour and did my best to imitate my mother's motions. I worked bits of leftover dough into patties with awkward hands and filled small pie tins with lopsided crusts. I squinted disapprovingly at the tins before pulling the dough from them to try again.

"You shouldn't roll pie dough more than once," my mother warned, "or it will become tough."

I collapsed in my chair in defeat. There were so many things I did not know and so many things I could not do! My mother made it all look easy.

I remember feeling similarly when years later, as a teenager, I lay on the living room couch reading a book after dinner. I didn't have much homework that night, and so I had some spare time on my hands. I knew the kitchen table needed clearing and that there was a pile of dishes in the sink.

"I should help," I remember thinking. Yet I continued to read my book. "I'm tired," I rationalized, "and besides, no one else is offering to help." I had eight siblings, after all. Why should I have to be the one who volunteered to help with dinner clean up?

I continued to lie there, reading my book, even as I noticed my mother rise from the kitchen table, where she always sipped a cup of tea after dinner, and begin to clear the table and wash the dishes by herself. She did not sigh or complain. She did not roll her eyes as I often did when called upon to help with extra chores. She simply got up and did what needed to be done.

I hated my lazy self in that moment, but not enough to actually get up and help. I lay there, staring at the pages of my book, and wondering at the kind of strength and generosity it takes to do small stuff like that—hidden, behind-the-scenes grunt work that others barely notice and that nobody even bothers to thank you for. The kind of thing I knew my mother did pretty much every moment of every day.

I thought of my mother's hands and the way they seemed so skilled at kitchen tasks and other jobs in the service of others. Washing, drying, scrubbing, folding, wiping, scraping, smoothing, and wringing out. These were things my hands still struggled to do.

My mother's hands were toughened from years of work. She could run them under hot water when washing bottles or pick up a hot casserole dish and barely feel it. My hands were sensitive and soft. I loathed my weakness in that moment, longing to be a better, tougher, stronger, more generous person. I considered my mother's hard work and generosity with awe, but it felt unattainable to me.

I was too selfish. Too soft. I could never give like that.

FINDING MY MOTHERHOOD

Years later, I leaned against a wall in the hospital hallway, breathing through contractions that ravaged my body with waves of unfamiliar pain.

"You're going to be OK," my husband Dan repeated over and over again, patting my shoulder gently. There was an edge to his voice, and I wasn't sure if he was trying to reassure me or himself (probably both of us). We were pretty new at this.

Months earlier, when I first stared in disbelief at two pink lines on a pregnancy test, I responded to the news by sitting on the bathroom floor and crying. Because this wasn't my plan. How is that for a natural mother?

I was clueless, but my body knew what to do. In the weeks that followed, I read pregnancy manuals with fascination, learning about the unique ways in which my body was adapting to accommodate a new life growing within me.

In all of my reading, there was no escaping an incredible truth: A human being! A unique, irreplaceable human being! That was what was growing inside of me!

Nausea rocked my body for the first three months, leaving me frail and underweight, and still my unborn baby thrived. As my belly grew, I dreamed of who my baby was. Who would he or she be? Would he like me? Would she have dark eyes? Would he play baseball? Would she love music?

The most surprising thing about that surprise first pregnancy was how, as immature and unprepared as I was, I readily shifted my focus from my own wants and needs to what would be best for the baby. I read all the books and stopped drinking diet soda, started eating more leafy, green vegetables, and stopped cleaning with chemicals.

I wasn't a perfect expectant mother, but I tried hard to be. And for the most part, I did not resent the imposition. It felt good to do what I knew in my heart I was supposed to do: take care of the tiny, dependent human being inside of me while my husband took care of me.

When at last my daughter was born, I cried tears of relief while the nurses cleaned her up and placed her on my chest. They undid her swaddling just a bit, telling me that "skin to skin" contact would be good for both of us. After months of touching on the inside, we touched for the first time on the outside, and it felt right.

"Her name is Kateri," I announced, still shaky from labor.

I looked at my daughter, and she looked straight back at me with bright, shining eyes that startled me with their alertness. She seemed to be taking it all in, this world she had been born into, this mother she had been given, and assessing its worth. Everything about her, from the softness of her skin to the dampness of her hair was fresh and clean. I remember thinking that she looked like she had been plucked from a garden, a tiny, new human being, fresh with budding promise, and placed in my waiting arms.

Everything about the experience of her birth, as painful and foreign an experience as it was, felt like it was meant to be. We had a baby. My husband was a father, and I was a mother. We were a nervous little family.

NOBODY TOLD ME

In the months that followed Kateri's birth, I found myself thinking and saying the words "Nobody told me!" quite a lot.

Nobody told me that starting to breastfeed could be so painful. Like tiny daggers in your flesh as your sweet baby seemingly sucked the very life from you.

Nobody told me that babies sometimes scream—loudly and all night long for no apparent reason.

Nobody told me that the sound of a baby's cries are uniquely designed to produce a stress response in other human beings, especially their mothers.

Nobody told me that sleep deprivation is a form of torture.

Nobody told me that the surge of hormones after birth would leave me weepy and confused at times, awake and profusely sweating in the middle of the night at other times, bewildered at my own rage sometimes, and then finally collapsing in a puddle of exhausted, grateful, joyful tears.

Nobody told me it would be so hard.

To be fair, though, they probably did. I just wasn't prepared to hear it. I could not grasp what an all-encompassing, life-altering thing motherhood could be until I experienced it for myself. My mother and my older sister did their best to talk me through some of the rougher stuff, but for the most part, I just had to keep up. My baby needed me, and just as my body did before she was born, I needed to adapt and grow.

I did grow. We went on to have more children, and as our family expanded, I marveled at the power our children have to change us. A parent-child relationship is a strange but natural kind of symbiosis. Our children need us to give to them, and we, somehow, find ourselves needing to give. So much it hurts.

I once read a description of motherhood that noted that when a nursing infant cries for milk, providing that milk provides relief for the mother as well as the child. Yes, they do suck the very life from us sometimes, and yet, somehow, we need them to do it. Physically, hormonally, emotionally, and spiritually, mothers especially are driven to give of ourselves for the good of our children.

Of course, that doesn't mean that we always do so perfectly, or that it is not a struggle sometimes, but most mothers recognize that the drive to give good things to their children, even at their own expense, is a natural one. It's built in.

THE FIRST WOMAN

You are probably familiar with the story of Adam and Eve. Most of us know Eve as the first woman, the first wife, and the first mother. You might have read the story of Creation and seen illustrations of the Garden of Eden in children's books when you were young. But who is this first woman, and what can we learn from her about God's plan for our womanhood? Let's take a fresh look at Eve's story now, with the eyes of grown women.

In the story of Creation, in the first chapter of Genesis, we read that God creates the first human beings, both male and female.

> So God created man in his own image, in the image of God he created him; male and female he created them. And God blessed them, and God said to them, "Be fruitful and multiply, and fill the earth and subdue it; and have dominion over the fish of the sea and over the birds of the air and over every living thing that moves upon the earth" (Genesis 1:27-28).

One thing that is clear in this simple description is the equality of men and women, in dignity, before God. Both men and women are made in God's image and likeness. Another important part of the story, however, is the fact that God created human beings as male and female. We are equal, but we are different. Our maleness and femaleness matter.

At the end of each day of Creation, God pronounces what he has made as "good," and after the creation of humans he does the same.

"And God saw everything that he had made, and behold, it was very good" (Genesis 1:31).

So we know that Adam and Eve were made in the image of God, equal in dignity before God; they were made different, and they were made good. In the next chapter, however, we read more intimate details about the creation of the first man and woman.

> Then the Lord God formed man of dust from the ground, and breathed into his nostrils the breath of life, and man became a living being ... Then the Lord God said, "It is not good that the man should be alone; I will make a helper fit for him" (Genesis 2:7; 2:18).

FLESH OF MY FLESH

In this further description, we begin to see more of the original unity of man and woman, the necessity of each, and their connection with one another. The connection between male and female, and the goodness of it, becomes even clearer in the passage that follows:

> So the Lord God caused a deep sleep to fall upon the man, and while he slept took one of his ribs and closed up its place with flesh; and the rib which the Lord God had taken from the man he made into a woman and brought her to the man. Then the man said, "This at last is bone of my bones and flesh of my flesh; she shall be called Woman, because she was taken out of Man." Therefore a man leaves his father and his mother and cleaves to his wife,

and they become one flesh. And the man and his wife were both naked, and were not ashamed (Genesis 2:21-25).

Here, we find out that the first woman was made from the very flesh of the first man; she at last is bone of his bones and flesh of his flesh. Adam does not name her Eve yet, but only "Woman," meaning she was taken from her man. Together, they are innocent—naked, without shame—and they share a beautiful, intimate form of unity. The two are one.

Men and women in their ideal state are made equal in dignity before God and are perfectly united with one another. But we all know the sad story that follows this illustrious beginning. Sin enters the Garden. Or a serpent, anyway, who brings temptation to the freshly made human beings.

DOUBTS CREEP IN

Earlier in this chapter, we read that God commanded the first man and woman not to eat the fruit of the Tree of Knowledge of Good and Evil, for if he does, he will die.

Now the serpent was more subtle than any other wild creature that the LORD God had made. He said to the woman, "Did God say, 'You shall not eat of any tree of the garden'?" And the woman said to the serpent, "We may eat of the fruit of the trees of the garden; but God said, 'You shall not eat of the fruit of the tree which is in the midst of the garden, neither shall you touch it, lest you die.' But the serpent said to the woman, 'You will not die. For God knows that when you eat of it your eyes will be opened, and you will be like God, knowing good and evil'" (Genesis 3:1-5).

These are lies, but the woman listens to them, ponders them in her heart, and begins to wonder if perhaps what the serpent says is true. The fruit of the tree looks good for eating. Perhaps God is not the good God he claims to be, after all, and he is only saving what is good for himself and keeping it from her and the man?

Doubting the goodness of God might be a familiar scene to you. When we choose sin of any kind, don't we make precisely the same calculation of distrust? We trust only in our own eyes to see and our own hands to take what we think is good, when we should instead trust in God to provide us with the good things we seek—security, pleasure, happiness, and joy.

After Adam and Eve disobey God and take what is not theirs, "the eyes of both [are] opened," we read, and they feel the shame of their sin. Next, we read God's description of what their sin will cost them.

> To the woman he said. "I will greatly multiply your pain in childbearing; in pain you shall bring forth children, yet your desire shall be for your husband, and he shall rule over you." And to Adam he said, "Because you have listened to the voice of your wife, and have eaten of the tree ... In the sweat of your face you shall eat bread till you return to the ground, for out of it you were taken; you are dust, and to dust you shall return" (Genesis 3:16-17, 19).

Pain, suffering, work, subjugation, and death. These are not happy things. Yet there, in the Garden, even as their unhappy state is described by God himself, Adam hears something hopeful. He hears a message not only of death, but of the possibility of new life: God says that the woman will have children.

Though he previously called her "Woman," now Adam gives his wife a new name, one that describes the hope she represents for their future. "The man called his wife's name Eve, because she was the mother of all the living" (Genesis 3:20).

Mother of all the living. Death is a new reality to the fallen man and woman, but Eve's promise of motherhood brings hope. Every woman's gift of motherhood is meant to be a source of goodness, hope, and joy.

EVERY WOMAN'S CALLING

Do you know that every woman has the gift of motherhood? By motherhood, of course, we do not necessarily mean the physical bearing of children, though that is the primary way many of us experience it. Motherhood, meaning the practice of feminine, nurturing love, can take many forms.

A teacher who gently guides a frustrated student is a mother. An aunt who watches her nieces and nephews after school is a mother. A CEO who treats her employees with compassion and understanding is a mother. A religious sister who feeds poor children in a third world nation is a mother. A woman who cares for her aging parents is a mother. A cashier at Walmart who seeks to resolve the disagreements of co-workers and remembers their birthdays with homemade treats is a mother. Of course, biological mothers, adoptive mothers, step-mothers, foster mothers, grandmothers, godmothers, and den mothers are all mothers too.

A call to motherhood, the practice of self-giving, nurturing love in all its feminine forms, is one that all women share in common. Like Eve before us, we are created different from men. We are made to make a gift of ourselves in service to the people God places in our lives. We are made for motherhood; it is a core part of our feminine identity.

St. John Paul II wrote and spoke eloquently about the differences between the sexes, and, in particular, the feminine gifts all women share. About the call to motherhood, he wrote:

> Motherhood is every woman's vocation, yesterday, today, always, it is her eternal vocation. A mother is one who understands everything and embraces each of us with her heart. Today's world is hungrier than ever for that motherhood, which, physically or spiritually, is woman's vocation as it was Mary's.[1]

Aren't these beautiful words? A mother "embraces each of us with her heart." Even if we have never read the writings of St. John Paul II, each of us can know the truth of these words in our hearts. We all know women who are skilled at making others feel uniquely known and loved by practicing the feminine arts of generosity, understanding, compassion, and sensitivity. We all know women, whether physical mothers or not, who notice the needs of others, especially the vulnerable, and teach others how to love and how to foster meaningful relationships with one another. This is motherhood. We all know the value of it in our hearts, when we see it and when we practice it.

I also love that St. John Paul II notes that "today's world is hungrier than ever for that motherhood." Isn't that the truth? You don't have to look any further than your Facebook newsfeed to know that the modern world needs the gift of feminine connection, nurturing, and love today more than ever.

---

[1] "Address of His Holiness John Paul II to the Young People Gathered in the Vatican Basilica," January 10, 1979.

There is hope in the goodness of our motherhood, and, like Eve who went before us into a world newly filled with death and sin, we are meant to bring that hope to others, even in a fallen world. We are meant to bless the world with our gift of self-giving, life-giving love.

THE PAIN OF MOTHERHOOD

Adam focused on the hopeful part of what God told Eve about the consequences of her sin, but perhaps you noticed a different part of the message? The part about multiplying pain in childbearing?

I used to think this part of Eve's "punishment" referred only to the physical pain women experience during labor, and that applies, but over the years, I have come to understand that it means so much more than that.

Yes, our motherhood is meant to be a gift to the world. Women are meant to bless the people God places in our lives with our feminine gifts of compassion, generosity, and life-giving, nurturing love. But motherhood costs us. It hurts— sometimes a lot.

There is the pain of pregnancy and childbirth, which is a form of suffering uniquely and tangibly attached to bringing forth new life. But then there is the incalculable "cost" of colicky nights, breast infections, toddler tantrums, health worries, growing pains, teenage anxiety, and a thousand hidden pains, losses, disappointments, discouragements, and thankless tasks in between.

Even before a woman knows she is pregnant, her body begins diverting nutrients and resources away from her own body in order to nurture the growing baby inside. This self-depleting, physical reality of womanhood mirrors a spiritual part of our feminine experience. We give even when it hurts.

For some women, the pain of motherhood takes the form of longing for a child that God never gives them or losing a child before birth, at birth, or long after. Or desperately loving a child with all we have only to have that child grow up and go astray or leave us lonely in our old age.

Sometimes the pain women experience in motherhood results from them pouring all they have into their marriage only to have it fall apart. It takes the form of giving to others in their home and workplace each day, in big and small ways, and not having that kindness reciprocated. For other women, this pain may come in the form of longing for friendship and love and finding only pain, misunderstanding, or rejection in their personal relationships.

But God sees us in our pain. He knows the unique ways that we suffer as women. His words to Eve in the Garden long ago still speak to us today. He speaks the truth about our motherhood and what it costs us. We bring forth children in great pain. That self-giving, life-giving love we women are made for sometimes hurts.

Yet those of us who practice motherhood, this uniquely feminine kind of self-giving love, know its worth. Whether or not our sacrifices are ever acknowledged or reciprocated, we know that it is inside of our connection with others and in giving of ourselves to others that we find meaning and value in anything we do.

This is why even women who accomplish great things in science, academics, or the arts, often point to their marriages, their children, and their families as their "greatest accomplishments" at the end of the day. Career women of all kinds regularly place the needs of children, parents, and others ahead of their professional goals, often at great cost to what some would consider worthy career goals.

And we know the worth of our motherhood, even when others fail to see it.

There is a woman at my parish who is a retired nurse. She once shared with me, as tears streamed down her face, the many times she stayed after hours to sit with elderly patients when they were very sick and close to death.

"My friends told me I was crazy, but they didn't have anyone," she told me, "and I couldn't leave them alone to die."

This woman, who never married and never had children of her own, mothered so many needy people with the gift of her presence in their last moments on earth. How many of us know quiet examples of generosity in motherhood like that?

GROWING INTO OURSELVES

I might never manage to roll a pie crust in quite the same way as my mom does, but I have grown in many ways since my younger years, thanks mostly to the sacrifices family life requires of me daily. I still have lazy, selfish moments where I don't quite relish the opportunities motherhood gives me to serve others with generosity and love, but I have learned to foster that feminine part of myself that is inclined to see the needs of others and give of myself by nurturing the people God has given me to love.

I have grown into my motherhood, and I am still growing— because I know the world needs my motherhood. And it needs yours, too.

Do you find satisfaction and fulfillment in your relationships with others? In what ways, conventional or unconventional, might God be calling you to "mother" the people in your life with a greater gift of yourself?

Do you ever let selfishness or insecurity get in the way of giving of yourself to others? Have you been wounded in your motherhood? Do you believe God sees you in your pain, knows the truth about the value of your sacrifice, and will fulfill your every longing in your relationship with him?

Are you ready to give others the gift of your motherhood, starting right now?

CLOSING PRAYER

Holy Spirit, giving life to all life, moving all creatures, root of all things, washing them clean, wiping out their mistakes, healing their wounds, you are our true life, luminous, wonderful, awakening the heart from its ancient sleep.

St. Hildegard of Bingen

Chapter Eight

GOD MADE YOU PERFECT

God Calls You to Greatness

STRIVING FOR PERFECTION

The baby was throwing up again. This wasn't just baby dribble; this was serious stuff. The doctor had called it "projectile" and prescribed Zantac for acid reflux. But I guess it wasn't working yet, because I found patches of baby puke in my hair, streaks running down the back of my shirt, and sweet, grinning baby Juliette in need of a complete change of clothes.

This was bad timing. I was trying to pull together my gang of little people to look at least a little bit presentable for a "family Mass" that was taking place at the Catholic school where my husband taught. I looked at my crew with their shirts coming untucked and hair falling loose from pigtails, and my stomach tightened. Students' and teachers' families gathered for this special occasion the school hosted once per year, and my memories of previous events told me that "perfect families" were going to be in attendance.

You know the kind. With dapper dads and stylish moms who wear artfully applied makeup. Their children's clothing matches, from floral dresses to bow ties with short pants. The little cherubs stand in perfect formation, hands neatly folded, angelic expressions on their faces. The babies of these families coo and flash gummy smiles; they charm onlookers with twinkling eyes. They do not throw up.

But my baby was still throwing up. After cleaning and changing her twice, I checked the time, panicked, and then rushed everyone out the door. Was my son wearing two left sneakers? Was my daughter sporting an orange Kool Aid moustache? No time for such trifling details now—we were late!

I drove to the church feeling a special kind of frazzled—a kind of frazzled I never knew as a young girl or even as a college student just five years earlier. I could handle the stress of running a cross-country race, taking final exams, or serving multiple tables as a waitress in a busy diner, but managing a young family had unearthed a special kind of anxiety in me I had not known previously.

I just wanted everything to be perfect. Was that too much to ask?

I wanted to be like the perfect moms I saw in those perfect families at church. I wanted everything to look good and everyone to behave themselves. I wanted to never run late, never get distracted, never be surprised by a mess, and never to feel like I was coming up short. Yet here I was, mom to a gang of small children, and these things seemed to happen to me every day. Especially today.

I blinked back tears as I drove. I imagined the perfect families who were surely already at the church, patiently waiting in the pews for Mass to begin. From the backseat, Juliette whimpered. I shushed her, and then she really began to cry. Long, loud wails filled our ears as we pulled into the parking lot.

My husband had saved us seats. He met us outside to help wrangle the kids out of their car seats and carry the sniffling, drooling baby—was that only drool? Yes, it was only drool—for now, anyway.

I was relieved to find that Mass had not started yet. We took our seats, Mass began, and then all became a blur. I had one of those Masses where I was so focused on my own appearance, my children's appearance, my children's behavior, and the seeming perfection of the people around me that I completely failed to pray.

I considered all the beautiful families, and especially the perfect moms, around me as I knelt in the pew. I recalled the senseless argument I had started with my husband that morning as he went out the door to work. I thought of the chaotic scene I had left at home that day, towels on the bathroom floor and dirty dishes piled high in the kitchen sink. I noticed my hair hanging in damp strands where I had rinsed it, still smelling faintly of baby puke.

I was a mess. I was a failure. I sat in the pew with my shoulders scrunched, my head down, and hot tears streaming down my face.

Are there "perfect" people in your life? Most of us knew at least a few girls who fit that description in high school, but the comparison games don't stop when we graduate. Any of us can fall prey to the temptation to turn others into idols and compare ourselves to a false idea of perfection at any stage in our lives. The "perfect" people you compare yourself to might be families at church, moms of your kids' friends, or co-workers who just seem to always have it all together.

When it comes to others, we notice the good stuff. You might notice that your sister's home is always neat and tidy, that your friend's kids never seem to bicker, or that your co-worker has a romantic husband.

When it comes to ourselves, though, we notice the bad stuff. We know all of our own dirt, don't we? The big stuff and the small stuff we don't want others to know or see:

My toddler won't stop picking his nose. My laundry is never caught up. My skin is breaking out. My husband is distant and moody. I scream at my kids. My teenager got caught shoplifting. I resent my mother-in-law's meddling. I'm worried my husband might be cheating. I'm worried about my mental health. I spend too much and have enormous credit card debt.

At the end of Mass that day, as the priests processed out of the church, one of them, a kind, older priest who knew our family well, paused at our pew, smiled at me gently, and then placed his hands on my shoulders and spoke the words of a blessing.

I'm sure he singled me out because I looked like such a needy mess, but in that moment, I did not feel embarrassed at all. I do not remember exactly what words he spoke, but for the first time since Mass began, I was not aware of how I looked or how my kids were behaving or what other people might be thinking. I was aware of only the goodness of God's love and the rush of relief I felt at knowing, tangibly, through the priest's simple touch and the words of his blessing, that I was loved. That I was good. That I was enough.

UNREAL PERFECTION

When it comes to the impossibility of perfection, we women are masters at finding ways to beat ourselves up with imaginary figures. Those women at church that day that I thought looked and acted so perfect? They were real people, and so they also were not perfect. Each of them was filled, I am sure, with her own list of flaws and failures and was focused on her own shortcomings, maybe even comparing herself to others around her—and coming up short.

What we fail to realize when we turn others into plastic perfect statues in our minds, is how dehumanizing that is. It turns others into objects, idols of perfection, rather than real, flesh and blood human beings with feelings, worries, thoughts, concerns, and unique challenges of their own. And it strips us of our dignity as real, flesh and blood human beings, uniquely created by God—flaws, puking babies, and all.

God made you perfect. That does not necessarily mean that you have perfect abs, a perfect career, the perfect marriage, or whatever other kind of perfection the magazine covers are shouting about these days. It means God made you perfectly suited to the life and work he has planned for you. He made you to be holy, and he calls you to greatness.

ANOTHER PERFECT WOMAN

All of this "call to greatness" stuff might sound a little intimidating, especially in light of those very real flaws and weaknesses we were just talking about and that we are all too aware of.

But God is not discouraged. He knows you, he knows your weaknesses, your flaws, and your failures inside and out, and he calls you anyway. He calls you because he knows the greatness you have in you. He put it there.

One seemingly "perfect" woman in the Bible is the woman we read about in Proverbs 31. Are you familiar with the "Proverbs 31" woman? She's kind of famous in Christian circles; she has many ministries named after her. Yet she can be a little bit of a divisive figure. Some women I know roll their eyes at the mere mention of the Proverbs 31 woman.

What a sad thing that is! Because that means that in Proverbs 31, they read a description of a powerful, generous, holy, wise, accomplished woman and hear in it an admonishment of those who fail to measure up to her lofty standards—which, let's face it, is all of us.

The Proverbs 31 woman sews like Betsy Ross: "She seeks wool and flax, and works with willing hands" (Proverbs 31:13).

She cooks like Martha Stewart: "She rises while it is yet night and provides food for her household and tasks for her maidens" (Proverbs 31:15).

She runs her business like Oprah: "The heart of her husband trusts in her, and he will have no lack of gain. She does him good, and not harm, all the days of her life" (Proverbs 31:11-12).

She gives like St. Teresa of Calcutta (Mother Teresa): "She opens her hand to the poor, and reaches out her hands to the needy" (Proverbs 31:20).

Here's the thing: Just like the perfection I imagined about those other women at Mass, just like the perfection you might imagine about your friend who just won Most Amazing Homemaker of the Year or the soccer mom who picks her son up at practice looking like a supermodel who just flew in from Milan, the perfection of the Proverbs 31 woman is not real.

It's not real! She's not real! And yet the Proverbs 31 woman is every one of us, and she is amazing.

I can explain.

What we read in Proverbs 31 is not a prescription for how every woman ought to live her life down to the details of spinning wool and sewing children's clothing. In fact, it is not a description of any real woman in particular. It is a beautiful poem of praise for womanly virtues. And guess what? You have those. God made you with them. They are built in.

The woman described in Proverbs 31 works hard in a variety of ways. She supports her husband, her children, and her home. She is organized and efficient; she works before the sun comes up and after it goes down, tirelessly serving others and giving to the poor.

Though our details might differ—no need to run out and buy a flock of sheep—we all are called to love, serve, and care for others in similar ways. This passage highlights and celebrates the unique ways that we women are capable of loving and giving to others. It honors womanly virtue and those of us who are gifted with it. Let's look at a few of the womanly gifts and strengths this chapter emphasizes.

GOD MADE YOU HARDWORKING

Reading through Proverbs 31 can leave you feeling exhausted. From dawn till dusk, this woman is *moving!* She spins her own wool and then makes clothing from it. She plants her own vineyard and then makes a profit from what she grows. She even makes her own coverlet—whatever that is!

While we may not be planting vineyards and weaving coverlets, if you are a woman, I know you work. What's more, you probably work most hours of most days in service to other people. Whether you are a mom, grandma, teacher, co-worker, helpful neighbor, or just a friend to those God puts in your life, you are uniquely qualified to serve those people with your own hard work.

This work is likely made up of a lot of little things you might not even notice.

The other day, my teenage son was sitting at the dining room table, working on his laptop. I walked by with a laundry basket, picking up stray socks along the way. I passed again, with a stack of dishes I picked up in the living room and loaded them in the dishwasher. I walked by a third time with clean towels I was putting away, and then finally, as I made a fourth pass by him, heading to the pantry to retrieve some items to prepare dinner, my son laughed out loud and asked, "Mom! Do you ever stop moving?"

I laughed myself because although I knew I had walked by several times doing different things, I had not even felt particularly busy. Yet we are busy. We are working hard, usually in the service of others, many hours of many days, and the description of the hardworking woman in Proverbs 31 offers praise and affirmation for that hard work we do.

It's hard work that comes naturally to women more readily than men. Men might be better suited to tasks requiring a great deal of strength or heavy lifting, but we women are really good at keeping up with the small stuff—all those little things that might go unnoticed until no one does them.

Sometimes we are tempted to belittle the value of the work we do because it seems so unglamorous. We wash sheets and wipe noses, we make stews and wipe counters, we swish toilets and empty trash cans, we fold laundry and fill soap dispensers. How can this be important stuff?

We know that it is. The "womanly work" of keeping households, workplaces, and whole communities running behind the scenes is not something that only women can do, and it is not something that only women *should* do, but it is something that women are uniquely good at. Seeing the small needs of others and taking action to take care of those needs is something Mary, the mother of Jesus, modeled for us in the Gospel story about the wedding at Cana.

Little things aren't trivial, demeaning, or meaningless. Little acts of service and attending to the needs of others is an active way of caring for others in ways that can make them

feel uniquely known and loved. That's no small thing—
that's everything!

GOD MADE YOU STRONG

Further in the passage, in Proverbs 31:17, we read that "She
clothes ... [herself] with strength and makes her arms strong."

This is a recognition of womanly strength. God made you
strong. Do you know your own strength?

Though men generally have greater physical strength
than women, every woman is uniquely equipped with the
emotional and spiritual strength she needs to nurture and
care for the people God places in her life. You have feminine
gifts that are unique to you and your circumstances. In chapter
three, we learned about Judith, who had the courage, cunning,
and strength to slay an enemy general. Here in Proverbs, we
are reminded that every woman has a gift of strength to share.

Do you persevere in the face of challenges? Do you refuse to
give up when a loved one needs you? Do you make personal
sacrifices of time, sleep, and money in service to the needs of
the people God has given you to love? Do you give of yourself
in sacrificial ways in order to show your love for others? These
are womanly gifts that we women practice in myriad ways.

But as we discussed in chapter 7, the ways in which we
women love others cost us—sometimes a lot. Remember what
we learned about the creation of the first woman, and the
universal feminine vocation to self-giving nurturing love? Not
only did God make you strong enough to meet the needs of
others, he made you uniquely capable of meeting the needs
of the people he gives you to love. No one can "mother" the
people in your life like you can. They need you and they need

your unique strength. The description of the strength of the Proverbs 31 woman recognizes and praises your strength.

GOD MADE YOU GENEROUS

Another feminine gift we find praised in Proverbs is generosity. "She opens her hand to the poor, and reaches out her hands to the needy" (Proverbs 31:20).

Do you remember St. John Paul II's description and praise of motherhood we read about in chapter seven? "A mother is one who understands everything and embraces each of us with her heart."

Women are uniquely gifted in the arts of sensitivity and of compassion, which lead to the gift of generosity. Have you ever noticed someone else's suffering, maybe even about something small, and reached out to that person in love?

That natural drive to truly "see" other people, alleviate their suffering, and care for our fellow human beings in physical and emotional ways is something that is written deeply in the heart of every woman. This does not have to take place on the streets of Calcutta for it to "count."

You might practice the feminine gifts of sensitivity and generosity in your workplace, where you notice a co-worker is feeling down and make an effort to cheer him or her up. You might practice it in your marriage, where you astutely monitor your husband's mood and take extra care to show him affection when he is struggling. You might practice it in your parenting, when you respond to a baby's cries, soothe a sick child, or counsel an anxious teen.

Just like the Proverbs 31 woman, wherever you are and in whatever circumstances God has placed you, you reach out your hands to the poor and extend your arms to the needy. Who are your poor and needy today? Who will you "embrace with your heart"? God affirms the dignity and worth of your calling through the words of praise for the feminine gifts of generosity we read included in Proverbs 31.

GOD MADE YOU FAITHFUL

The most important words of praise we read in the description of the woman in Proverbs 31, though, are not praise for her hard work, strength, or generosity. They are praise for her faithfulness. "Strength and dignity are her clothing, and she laughs at the time to come" (Proverbs 31:25).

She laughs at the days to come! Do you laugh at the days to come? I know I sometimes cry about the days to come, or lie awake at four in the morning, worrying about them.

Here in these words, though, we hear our true call to greatness as women made in the image and likeness of God. Here is where we find out what kind of women God really made us to be—women who trust in God's goodness and love. Women who look to the future without fear. Women of confident faith.

The final words of this passage sum it all up for us: "Charm is deceitful, and beauty is vain, but a woman who fears the LORD is to be praised. Give her the fruit of her hands, and let her works praise her in the gates" (Proverbs 31:30-31).

The woman who fears the Lord is to be praised. And that is precisely what Proverbs 31 is doing. Praising the woman. Praising her for who she is and who God made her to be. Praising her for the greatness God calls her to. That means you. And that means me.

If you are ever tempted to compare yourself to other women—their looks, their relationships, their work, and their accomplishments—remember the Proverbs 31 woman and what the true source of praise is for her. She is a "woman of worth" not because of any good works she does, but because she believes and trusts in the Lord and knows who God made her to be—his beloved daughter. And that's who you are, too.

It is worth noting that there is only one other woman in the Old Testament who is described with such high praise as a "woman of worth." Remember Ruth? We met her in chapter 6 when we talked about the gift of sisterhood. Ruth was the widowed woman who stayed faithful to her mother-in-law, Naomi, despite the fact that she was left destitute and starving herself. Boaz noted her faithfulness and generosity, praised her for her loyalty, and called her a "woman of worth."

These words of highest praise were bestowed on Ruth despite the fact that she was unmarried, had no children, had no household to run, did not plant a vineyard, and owned neither loom nor flocks. She was a "woman of worth" because of her faithfulness, not because of anything she owned or accomplished.

The accomplishments listed in Proverbs 31 are meant only as a description of praise for feminine gifts and strengths. They are not a specific standard of perfection or a detailed to-do list held up to admonish any woman who fails to compare. They are simply praise for the great gift of womanhood, motherhood, and feminine faithfulness.

Finally, it is worth noting that there are no words of command directed toward female readers of Proverbs 31. Some women read this passage and feel they are being told what to do, but this is not the case. The only order given in the entire passage is in the final, most emphasized words, the climactic end of the poem. The command is given only to men and to children, directing them to praise their wives and mothers:

"Her children rise up and call her blessed; her husband also, and he praises her ... Give her the fruit of her hands, and let her works praise her in the gates" (Proverbs 31:28, 31).

In fact, many Jewish families practice the custom of singing the words of Proverbs 31, or *Eshet Hayil*, as a way of honoring their wives and mothers, giving thanks for their hard work in service to their families. We, too, should hear in these words a song of praise and thanksgiving, an ode to the wonderful gift of woman.

The Proverbs 31 woman does not come to tell you all the ways that you are falling short. She does not come to set some impossible standard for perfection that none of us will ever measure up to. She does not come to tell you that you are not enough.

The Proverbs 31 woman comes to tell you that you—exactly as God made you—are enough. More than that, you are a gift. You are beautifully and wonderfully made. God made you strong, loving, generous, and faithful. God made you good. Thanks be to God for the gift of you.

CLOSING PRAYER

Go forth in peace, for you have followed the good road. Go forth without fear, for he who created you has made you holy, has always protected you, and loves you as a mother. Blessed be you, my God, for having created me.

St. Clare of Assisi

CONCLUSION

When I was a young mom, we were fortunate to live close to Dan's paternal grandmother. Effie Bean, "Great Grammy Bean" to my young kids, lived about thirty minutes away. Grammy was a tough old New Englander who insisted upon living by herself in her own small home well past her ninetieth birthday, but she loved it when I would bring the kids to visit for an afternoon.

We would pour glasses of lemonade and sit on her front porch, watching the kids pick dandelions and breathing in the heavy scent of lilac bushes nearby. Then I would ask Grammy questions.

I asked about her wedding day. I asked about the birth of each of her kids. I asked about the work she used to do in the factory. I asked about raising kids without electricity or running water. I asked about getting around in the days before she had a car. I asked about dates she went on with her husband back when they were "courting." I asked about all the details, the big things and the small things, that had made up her long life so far.

Grammy would always patiently share funny stories, everyday stories, and tragic stories from long ago, but she often would pause before answering, scrunch up her face just a bit, and say, "That was a long time ago. Why do you care about all this old stuff, anyway?"

I cared because her stories were real. They were history. They were my kids' roots.

I cared because the stories she told underscored the timelessness of the human experience. People worked and prayed. They fell in love, got married, and had babies. They suffered loss, struggled through hard times, and learned and grew along the way.

We are still doing all that stuff.

In today's world of instant sharing and multiple forms of digital "connection," too often something is lost. When everything is instant, few things feel permanent. In a world where everything feels fleeting and temporary, we are made for everlasting life; we are meant to experience God's abiding love.

One of the times I visited with Grammy, she took out an old photo album and we paged through it together, pausing so I could ask questions and she could tell stories about the people in the faded photographs inside.

Toward the end, Grammy handed me a photo of a woman seated and wearing a high-necked, long-sleeved, ruffled dress. "Ella De Witt" was scrawled on the back of the photo in Grammy's unmistakable handwriting. Ella De Witt was Grammy's grandmother on her father's side, she explained. This was an extra copy, and so I could keep it if I wanted.

I had the photo framed and hung it on the wall in our living room. It still hangs there today. I cherish this photo because it reminds me that while I might not share blood with Ella De Witt, or even with Effie Bean, I share stories with them. Shared stories are the stuff that gives life lasting meaning.

Here in this book, we have shared even older stories, ones that come from the ancient chapters of the Bible itself, with all the timelessness that implies. In them, I have found, and I hope you have, too, a timeless message of God's abundant and unique love for each of us.

Through the stories of Rahab and Abigail, we see that God calls each of us in unique ways, and ultimately, we find our place of true belonging only inside of our relationship with him. *God calls you just as you are.*

In the experiences of Bathsheba and Tamar, we learn that even when others do not, God sees us in our pain, loves us as his precious daughters, and longs to heal our wounds. *God acknowledges your suffering and lifts you up.*

Through the stories of Judith and Delilah, we learn that women have unique strength in this world, and that God gives us the freedom to use our gifts to bless those around us. *God gives you power to do great things and the freedom to choose.*

In the stories of Hannah and Sarah, we find encouragement and hope in knowing that God never abandons us. He cares deeply about the things we pray for and wants to give us good things. *God knows the desires of your heart, and they are good.*

When we read the stories of the widow of Zarephath and the Shunammite woman, we are reminded of our call to trust in God for all things. We are all dependent upon God for all things; he will provide for us, even through the toughest of times. *God knows your needs and promises to take care of you.*

Through the stories of Miriam, the Pharaoh's daughter, Ruth, Naomi, Rachel, and Leah, we learn about the gift of feminine friendship and the call to support and encourage one another in the unique challenges we face as women. *God gives you the gift of friendship and connection with others.*

In the story of Eve, we find out about the universal call to motherhood, the unique gifts and strengths God gives us as women, and the ways in which we are called to fulfill our greatest purpose by loving and nurturing others. *God blesses others with the gift of you.*

Finally, in the story of the woman in Proverbs 31, we learn that we are all called by God in different ways. God made each of us perfect for the role he wants us to play in our families, in our communities, and in our world at large. *God calls you to greatness.*

Through the power of these ancient stories, I hope you can begin to see the timelessness of God's infinite love, to trust in his goodness, and to let go of all the things that don't matter.

God loves you just as you are.

God calls you just as you are.

Find courage to stop struggling for love. Find strength to stand on the shoulders of our sisters who went before us and be fully and authentically yourself. Find the joy you are meant to have as the precious daughter of a God who knows you and loves you inside and out.

Standing on the strength of our shared stories, let the truth of God's abiding love speak directly to your heart, and accept the message he speaks to you there.

God made you good, and you are enough. Thanks be to God for the gift of you.

A Completely **Unique Bible** that Brings Salvation History to Life

With commentary from the creator of The Great Adventure, *Jeff Cavins, and renowned Scripture scholars Mary Healy, Andrew Swafford, and Peter Williamson*

Every Catholic needs this Bible! *The Great Adventure Catholic Bible* makes the complexity of reading the Bible simple. The narrative approach gives the big picture of salvation history and shows how everything ties together. This is the only Bible that incorporates *The Great Adventure's* color-coded *Bible Timeline*™ Learning System, a system that has made *The Great Adventure* the most popular and influential Bible study program in the English-speaking world. The color-coded tools make it easy to read and easy to remember. Truly a "game changer"! There has never been another Bible like it.

Find **Peace, Balance,** and **Joy**
in Your Vocation as a Mother

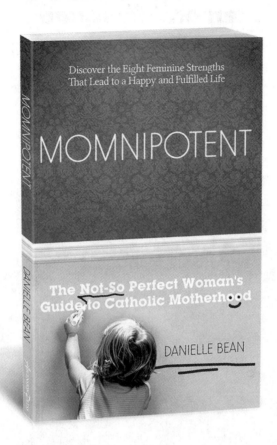

Discover the Eight Feminine Strengths
That Lead to a Happy and Fulfilled Life

MOMNIPOTENT

The Not-So Perfect Woman's
Guide to Catholic Motherhood

DANIELLE BEAN

*Momnipotent: The Not-So-Perfect
Woman's Guide to Catholic Motherhood*

In *Momnipotent,* Danielle Bean provides much-needed encouragement to all women and validates the dignity and importance of motherhood. She helps mothers recognize eight uniquely feminine strengths and how to use those strengths to find peace, purpose, balance, and joy in being the women God created and called them to be. This book is part of an Ascension study program by the same name.

Listen and Respond Like
Mary at the Annunciation

Annunciation by Giovanni Battista Teipolo (1725)

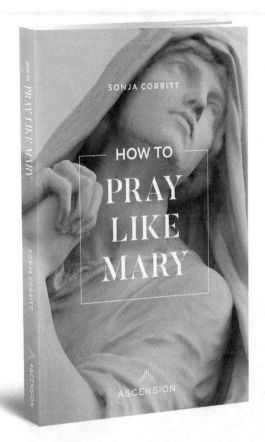

How to Pray Like Mary by Sonja Corbitt

Mary has been called the "mother of listening." She didn't just *hear* the Word—she knew *how to hear it* in light of her own relationships, circumstances, and habits—and then let it transform her. In *How to Pray Like Mary*, Sonja Corbitt presents the Blessed Mother as the ultimate prayer guide in a powerful "listening" practice: **L**isten, **O**bserve, **V**erbalize, **E**ntrust. Drawn from vivid biblical texts such as Hannah's song, the Psalms, and the Annunciation, this book reveals how to surrender to the Spirit and pray the Scriptures as Mary did.